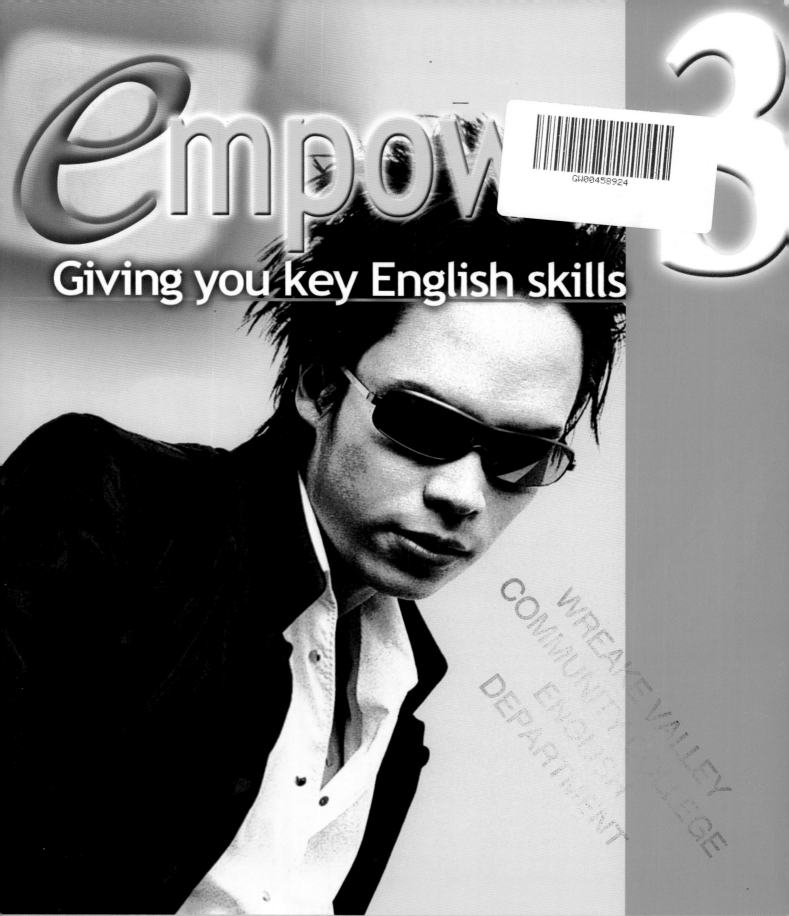

empow3

Giving you key English skills

WREAKE VALLEY COMMUNITY COLLEGE ENGLISH DEPARTMENT

 Steve Eddy    Lucy English   Mary Green

FOLENS

Acknowledgements

Approximately 250 words from MACB by Neil Arksey (Puffin, 1999) Copyright © Neil Arksey, 1999.

Kit's Wilderness by David Almond (Signature, 1999).

The Fourteenth Summer by Gary Paulsen (Macmillan Children's Books, 1993). Reproduced by permission of Macmillan Publishers, London.

Black Elk Speaks: Being the Life Story of a Holy Man of the Oglala Sioux as told through John G. Neihardt (Flaming Rainbow) by Nicholas Black Elk (University of Nebraska Press, 2000).

The Wonderful Adventures of Mrs Seacole in Many Lands by Mary Seacole, edited by Ziggi Alexander and Audrey Dewjee (Falling Wall Press, 1984).

'Frolics with Phantoms' by Neil del Strother from The Big Issue, Issue 461, October – November 2001.

'Baseball Cap' by Faithless, lyrics by Maxi Jazz from the album Reverence. © Champion Records/BMG/Warner Chappell.

'Highland Ox' by Paul Sparkes from Apple Fire selected by Jill Pirrie (Bloodaxe Books, 1993).

'Goodnight Stroud' by Pie Corbett from The Apple Raid selected by Pie Corbett (Macmillan Children's Books, 2001).

'Seaside Sonata' by Mary Green. © Mary Green. First published in *Are We Nearly There Yet?* Poems chosen by Brian Moses (Macmillan, 2002).

'Balloons' by Sylvia Plath from *Collected Poems* by Sylvia Plath (Faber and Faber, 1981). Reproduced by permission of the publishers, Faber and Faber. 13 lines from BEOWULF Anon. translated by Michael Alexander (Penguin Classics, 1995). Copyright © Michael Alexander, 1995.

Photos: pp 11, 65, 93, 133 – REX Features; pp 59, 60, 134 – Digital Vision; 61, 66, 69, 74 – Corel; pp 87, 89, 90 – Columbia Tristar / PAPicselect; pp 111, 118, 134 – Eyewire Inc.; pp 121, 141 – The Kobal Collection; p 21 – David F. Barry / Corbis; p 22 – Hulton Archive / Getty Images; p 27 – Digital Stock; p 32 – Foodpix / Getty Images; p 47 – Bubbles Photo Library; p 67 – PhotoDisc; p 71 – Morton Beebe / Corbis; p 83 – Legoland; pp 106, 117 – Donald Campbell; p 128 – The Vintage Magazine Company.

© 2003 Folens Limited, on behalf of the authors.

United Kingdom: Folens Publishers, Apex Business Centre, Boscombe Road, Dunstable, LU5 4RL.
Email: folens@folens.com
Ireland: Folens Publishers, Greenhills Road, Tallaght, Dublin 24.
Email: info@folens.ie
Poland: JUKA, ul. Renesansowa 38, Warsaw 01-905.

Editor: Sara Wiegand
Layout artist: Patricia Hollingsworth
Cover design: Duncan McTeer
Design: FMS Design
Illustrations: Ivan Allen, Roger Courthold, Karen Perrins, Tony Randell and Lee Sullivan

First published 2003 by Folens Limited.

British Library Cataloguing in Publication Data. A catalogue record for this publication is available from the British Library.

ISBN 1 84303 283-X

Your questions answered

Q: I really want to improve my work in English. How is *Empower 3* going to help me?

A: *Empower* is a new series designed to help you progress in a range of English skills. At the same time it gives you stimulating and interesting texts to read. The authors are experienced English teachers, examiners and writers – so they know just what you need.

Q: Why is it in six sections?

A: Each section deals with a vital part of English including areas such as Media and ICT texts, as well as non-fiction materials. In addition, there is a special section, 'Preparing for Assessment' to help you tackle the end of Key Stage 3 assessment you will have to face.

Q: How is it different from other books I have used in English?

A: Each Unit sets out a very clear process for you to follow.
- 'Let's investigate' tells you what area of English you are going to look at.
- 'Starting points' provides you with a quick 'warm-up' task on a useful skill.
- 'Reading' deals with an interesting text written by a professional writer.
- 'Reading focus' asks you some basic questions to make sure you have understood.
- 'Modelling writing' shows you how you can write in the same way.
- 'Summary' reminds you at the end of key points worth remembering.

Q: But what about these other sections, 'Challenge', 'Spelling Zone' and 'ICT Zone'?

A: The 'Challenge' task is exactly what it says. If you have managed the work in the Unit, try your hand at this task – you're ready for it!

The 'ICT zone' gives you the opportunity to do some new work on the Web, or using a well-known programme, such as 'Word'.

The 'Spelling zone' is a regular feature to keep you on track to improve your spelling.

Q: And what's this 'Profile' at the end of each section?

A: This is simply a record of what you have covered in the section – if you have done all the work. Your teacher should have a copiable version of this that they can fill in and pass to you to show your parents, friends, or other school teachers.

Q: Is there any other support for my English work?

A: There is a CD that is available with the book. This provides:
- a range of cut-out skills cards to paste into your file or book
- writing frames to help you organise your writing (see the *(f)* icon in the book)
- profiles for your teacher to complete and print out
- quick starter activities
- PowerPoint presentations for you to complete and present.

Enjoy your work!

Contents

Writing outcomes	PowerPoint Presentations	Key focus
Imagine, explore, entertain *Inform, explain, describe*	Aim: to show how writers can make writing 'come to life'.	Analysing structure, narrative, perspective and writers' viewpoints. Exploring the ways non-fiction texts entertain.
Inform, explain, describe *Argue, persuade, advise*	Aim: to create a persuasive and informative presentation.	Explore presentational devices in non-fiction texts. Use counter-arguments in persuasive writing.
Imagine explore, entertain	Aim: to present a range of poems in PowerPoint form.	Explore how form contributes to meaning. Analyse traditions and cultural contexts for poetry. Consider authorial perspective in poetry.
Analyse, review, comment *Argue, persuade, advise*	Aim: to explore the key features of advertisements.	Analyse presentational devices in media texts. Explore persuasive and informative devices in texts.
Imagine, explore, entertain *Analyse, review, comment*	Aim: to prepare for the Shakespeare paper in the Key Stage 3 test.	Compare different interpretations of plays by different dramatists. Convey a variety of dramatic techniques when scripting plays.
n/a	Aim: to learn about the different types of questions you might face in tests.	Transferring skills from classroom to test. Preparing for Key Stage 3 test assessment and beyond.

A1 Introduction

Let's investigate...

- How close are fiction and non-fiction?

Objectives	
Word	
Sentence	7
Reading	
Writing	6, 11
Speaking/Listening	

▶ Starting points: literary writing

Remember...

Words give you power. As a writer you can:
- describe characters' actions and reactions
- explain things to the reader
- use dialogue to show character and how a situation develops
- use descriptive vocabulary to make the reader imagine
- express views and values.

To show how much power you have as a writer, look how you can bring something simple to life by adding description, action, explanation and dialogue.

the man ⟶ the *young* man ⟶ the young man *in the shabby coat* ⟶

the young man in the shabby coat *held out* ⟶

the young man in the shabby coat held out *the small baby* ⟶

the young man in the shabby coat held out the small baby. ⟶

'Take her,' he pleaded ...

1.1

Now do the same with 'the girl'. Add an adjective, a phrase, an action, another detail and some dialogue/speech.

the girl ⟶

6

All the units in this section will show you the skills that writers use, how you can identify them and, most importantly, how you can use them yourself. These new skills include:

writing to build up to a climax

describing and commenting on events

keeping the reader guessing

comparing extracts by different writers

using different narrative viewpoints.

People have different viewpoints.

You will have already discussed the difference between 'literary' and 'non-literary' writing.

You will have also thought about how fiction and non-fiction can be quite similar. As you read the extract on page 8, think about whether this story is like a 'made-up' story.

Reading: what is literature?

In this short extract, Ernest Shackleton describes a 16-day boat journey to find help for his troubled Antarctic expedition.

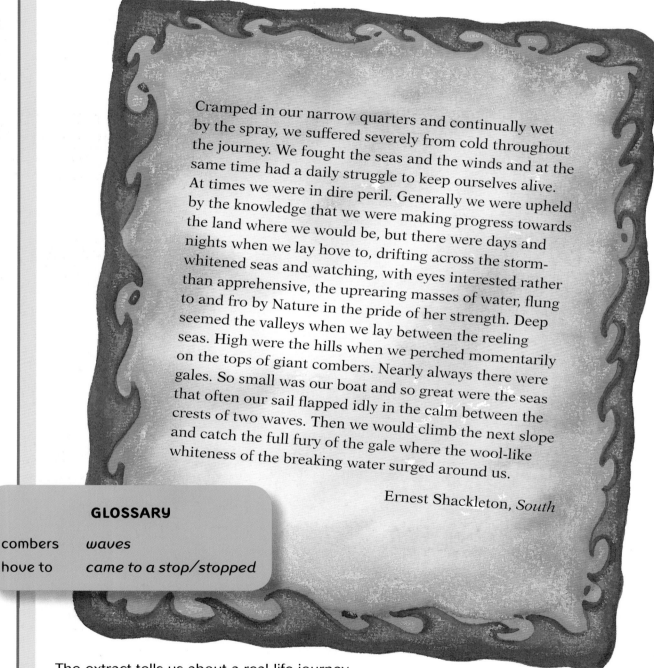

Cramped in our narrow quarters and continually wet by the spray, we suffered severely from cold throughout the journey. We fought the seas and the winds and at the same time had a daily struggle to keep ourselves alive. At times we were in dire peril. Generally we were upheld by the knowledge that we were making progress towards the land where we would be, but there were days and nights when we lay hove to, drifting across the storm-whitened seas and watching, with eyes interested rather than apprehensive, the uprearing masses of water, flung to and fro by Nature in the pride of her strength. Deep seemed the valleys when we lay between the reeling seas. High were the hills when we perched momentarily on the tops of giant combers. Nearly always there were gales. So small was our boat and so great were the seas that often our sail flapped idly in the calm between the crests of two waves. Then we would climb the next slope and catch the full fury of the gale where the wool-like whiteness of the breaking water surged around us.

Ernest Shackleton, *South*

GLOSSARY

| combers | *waves* |
| hove to | *came to a stop/stopped* |

The extract tells us about a real-life journey.
But it is literary because it gives us more than the bare facts.
It uses imaginative language. For example: *'We fought the seas … '*. This does not mean a fist-fight; it tells us what a struggle it was for the six men in the boat.

Reading focus: have you understood?

1.2

The writer helps us to imagine how he felt by using powerful images. What is unusual or powerful about each of these?

'Deep seemed the valleys ... '

'Nature in the pride of her strength ... '

'the storm-whitened seas ... '

'the wool-like whiteness of the breaking water surged around us'.

Writing: modelling how it's done

1.3 (f)

Your turn!

Think of an ordeal (a difficult experience) you have gone through. Make notes on how you would describe and comment on your ordeal so that readers would know what it was like. Follow this framework:

1. Explain what the ordeal was, and why it was hard for you.

2. Write a sentence containing at least one good adjective to describe what it was like.

3. Write a sentence containing an image helping readers to imagine what it was like. (An image is a word picture; for example, the words *'wool-like'* compare the sea with wool.)

Summary

- Non-fiction and fiction can be very similar (see page 7).
- Words give you power as a writer (see page 9).
- One feature of literary writing is that it appeals to the reader's imagination (see page 9).

A2 The big build-up ▶ ▶ ▶

A2 The big build-up

Let's investigate...

- How do writers build up to a climax?
- What is a 'twist' in a plot or story?

▶ Starting points: formal and informal

Your written or spoken English can be **formal** or **informal**, depending on the situation. Here are some examples:

- **Formal**: interviews for jobs, speeches, serious books, letters to strangers.
- **Informal**: chatting with a friend, funny books, notes, text messages, etc.

In a formal situation, you generally use standard English.
In an informal situation you can use a more relaxed style. You could even use slang or dialect (local) words.

2.1

Make the sentences below more formal.

For example: He's off his trolley = He's mad.

> Do that again and we'll have you.

> You're dead! (to someone who has stolen your bag)

> He was doing all right till he got cocky.

> I'm right knackered.

> She's scarpered.

As you will see, the following extract uses informal speech.

Reading: action and climax

Gregg's kick came soaring high over the field. Mac had dropped back to help with the defence; now he powered up the field in front of the midfielders. Banksie was way out in front.

'Go on, Banksie!' yelled Mac. 'Run with it – take it all the way!'

Bringing the ball under control, Banksie began to accelerate. Slightly ahead of him, two defenders shadowed his every twist and swerve. They were the only players between him and the keeper; they seemed determined he shouldn't get past.

They were big for defenders and incredibly solid, given their speed. In the first half they had made sure he discovered that the hard way. Previous clashes had been bruising.

'Don't get cocky now, blondie.' The bigger of the two dropped a shoulder and barged him, hard. 'We don't like cocky,' he grunted.

Banksie shoved back.

Scarface, to his left, barged harder. 'You're for it!'

Slamming on the brakes, Banksie cut back and ran wide. The rest of the field were closing the gap. The wrong-footed defenders snarled and cursed. Now was the moment.

He charged for the goal, a heat-seeking missile locked on target. All he had to do was stay ahead and shoot. He had the edge – he was wide, but there was nothing between him and the keeper.

'You're ours, blondie.'

'This time we're having you.' Above the sound of his own gasping breath, his own thumping blood and pounding feet, he could hear them, centimetres behind.

'You've pushed us too far!'

'You're dead!'

He was close enough to tap it, but travelling too fast …

'Bye-bye, blondie.'

'It's been fun …'

'Aaaaaaagh!' Pain ripped through his legs.

The ground leapt up and smashed him in the face.

Neil Arksey, *MacB*

Reading focus: have you understood?

2.2

Talk about the questions below with a partner. Then write your answers on your own.

- What happens in the extract? Sum it up.
- Who encourages Banksie to run with the ball?
- What image is used for Banksie as he's just about to score?
- Why does the defender say, *'It's been fun …'*?

Writing: modelling how it's done ▶ ▶ ▶

Writing: modelling how it's done

The extract is full of action and builds up to a climax right at the end.
This is the end of a chapter, but a short story could even end like this – with a bang!

Questions, such as the ones in 2.2, are similar to those you will be asked in your Key Stage 3 tests. They deal with different things:
- **Who and what**: the basic events and story.
- **The language**: how the writer gets the story across.
- **Explanation**: why a word or phrase is used.

How the writer does something is the real key.
For example, notice the stages of the build-up:
1. Banksie gets his break.
2. The two defenders are introduced, just as a small detail at first.
3. We hear that they are big and 'solid', but fast.
4. They threaten Banksie menacingly.
5. The 'twist' – Banksie loses them and almost reaches the goal.
6. They catch up and threaten him again.
7. They trip him and he falls.

Notice, too, how the short sentences at the end speed things up.

2.3 *f*

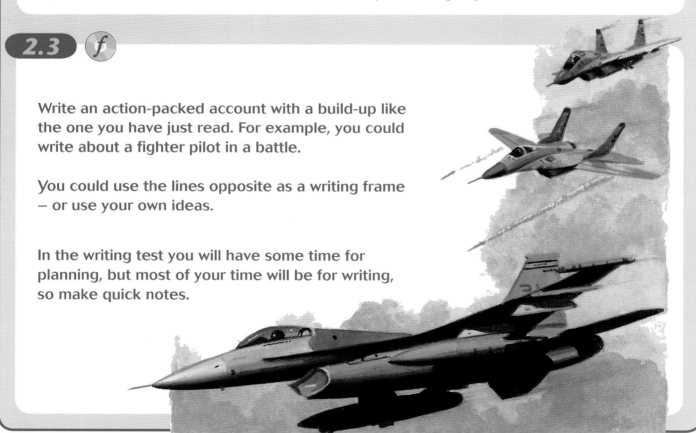

Write an action-packed account with a build-up like the one you have just read. For example, you could write about a fighter pilot in a battle.

You could use the lines opposite as a writing frame – or use your own ideas.

In the writing test you will have some time for planning, but most of your time will be for writing, so make quick notes.

In this example, the writer describes the fighter pilot's actions.

The situation is introduced: *He let out the throttle and settled into his seat …*
The problem occurs: *Two small dark shapes emerged from the clouds behind him. It was …*
Something happens: *Two streaks of fire leapt across the sky from either side …*
Reaction: *He banked steeply and lost sight of them …*
A new problem, or twist …? *This time the missiles were on target …*

Improving your work

2.4

When you have done a draft, check that you have:

- **used proper sentences**, beginning with a capital and ending with a full-stop
- **used standard English**, except in any speech
- **used shorter sentences** as you near the climax
- **used a build-up** like the one in the story.

Challenge: spotting connections

2.5

The football extract is from a novel based on Shakespeare's play *Macbeth*.
In the play, Macbeth feels that his friend Banquo has become a threat. Macbeth encourages Banquo to go out riding, then arranges to have him murdered by some desperate men, who kill him on his way back.

- What connections can you see between the play and the extract?
- If you are studying *Macbeth*, can you find a scene, or part of the play, when Macbeth hears some bad news?
- Now find the scene where he deals with this bad news (usually murderously). Note both of these scenes down.

Summary

- You can build up action to an exciting climax, with a twist (see page 12).
- Your English can be formal or informal, depending on the situation (see page 10).
- Short sentences can speed the account up (see page 12).
- Links can be made between different scenes and texts (see page 13).

A3 Points of view

Let's investigate...

- How can writers deal differently with a similar incident?
- What is narrative viewpoint?

Objectives	
Word	1
Sentence	3
Reading	7
Writing	5
Speaking/Listening	

▶ Starting points: active and passive sentences

Writers use **active** and **passive** sentences for different purposes. **Active** sentences use a verb (doing word) in its active form:

> A bear grabbed the baby.

Passive sentences use a verb in its passive form:

> The baby was stolen by a bear.

Both are correct, but the active form often sounds better if you need to sound direct and dynamic. The **passive** form can also suggest someone not being in charge:

> I was taken and experimented on by aliens.

You can also use the **passive** form if it is unclear *who* has done something (for example, in a news report):

> The window had been smashed.

3.1

Change the active sentences into passive sentences, and the passive ones into active. Some have been started for you.

- A horse kicked him. **Answer**: *He was …*
- Responsibility for the bomb has not been claimed by anyone. **Answer**: *No one …*
- He was woken by the snarling.
- The bear knocked him sideways.
- I was landed on by somebody.
- My boyfriend just dumped me.

As you read the two extracts, notice whether sentences are active or passive. What effect, if any, do these sentences have on the reader?

Reading: narrative viewpoint

The following two extracts both involve bears. The first is set in the Stone Age, the second in modern times.

Extract 1

The snarling woke him, then the sound of his mother's screams. Lak gripped the stone axe in his fist. He saw the huge silhouette of the bear in the entrance to the cave. The dying embers of the fire reflected in its eyes. His brothers and sisters cowered against the inner wall. His mother stood before them, her arms outstretched, protecting them. His father crouched low, a rock in his fist. The bear snarled again. It lurched further in, its great paws raised, the great claws glistening. The cave was filled with the stench of its breath. His father leapt from the shadows, struck the bear's head with his rock. The bear swept him aside and he lay unmoving on the earth. Now Lak sprang forward. He caught the beast between the eyes with his axe. He struck again at the bear's arm as it came towards him. He tried to strike again but the bear threw him back against the wall. The children whimpered and screamed. Lak struck the bear's back. He stretched high and struck its head again. His father stirred, yelled at the beast. He flung the rock and it struck the bear's shoulder. Lak struck again – the arm, the neck, the head again. The bear roared and bellowed as it reached down, knocked Lak's mother aside, grabbed one of his sisters by the deerskin that swaddled her and lifted her and carried her out into the night.

David Almond,
Kit's Wilderness

Continued ▶ ▶ ▶

Extract 2

Everything ended when he landed on the bear. He had seen them before, seen them in the mountains, and knew they could take a terrible toll of sheep. But he had always thought of them as almost cute, like pets, and slow and plodding.

He could not believe how fast this bear moved. He wasn't a large bear – perhaps three hundred pounds – but he was a very mad bear. All he wanted was a few sheep and dogs had come from all directions, snapping at him, and then a horse came out of the night and nearly ran over him and somebody shot at him and then that same somebody flew through the air and landed on him.

He seemed to turn inside his skin, shifted beneath John, rolled and came to his back legs just as John landed, half on his feet.

The bear swung sideways with its right paw. One sweeping hook and it caught John on the left shoulder.

'Ooofff!'

He'd never been hit so hard. Even getting kicked by a horse in the stomach had not been this hard.

He almost literally flew sideways and all still at once, almost at once. Off the horse, the rifle shot, onto the bear, knocked sideways all in less than a second.

A ball, he thought. He'll come after me, try to finish me. Roll in a ball and try to get through it.

Gary Paulsen, *The Fourteenth Summer*

 Reading focus: have you understood?

3.2

Talk about the questions below with a partner. Then write your answers on your own.

- What do the two extracts have in common?
- Suggest two ways in which they are different.
- How can you tell when in history each extract is set?
- What happened in extract 2?
- How does extract 2 appeal to the reader's senses of sight, hearing and smell?
- Why does the writer of extract 2 sometimes use incomplete sentences – for example in the last paragraph?

Spelling zone: changing vowel sounds

Vowels (a e i o u) can make either a short or a long sound, as can be seen in the extract.

Short sound: **fat**   **grip**   **shin**   **slop**

Long sound: **fate**   **gripe**   **shine**   **slope**   (The 'e' at the end lengthens the sound.)

A long 'e' sound is usually made by 'ea' or 'ee': beat sweet

To keep a long vowel sound with 'ing', you have to drop the 'e':

gripe → griping   **shine → shining**   **hope → hoping**   **slope → sloping**

If you want a short vowel sound with 'ing', double the last letter before adding 'ing':

grip → gripping   **win → winning**   **slop → slopping**   **slug → slugging**

Writing: modelling how it's done

Narrative viewpoint means through whose eyes the story is told.
Some stories are told in the 'first person':

The snarling awoke me … I landed on the bear.

However, both of these extracts are written in the 'third person' (*'He …'*) , but mostly from the boy's viewpoint in each case.

In extract A the writer focuses on what Lak heard, saw and smelled – not anyone else.

What other viewpoints could he have chosen?

In extract B, the sentence beginning *'All he wanted was a few sheep …'* is different.
Whose viewpoint is this?

One way to show viewpoint is to suggest a character's thoughts. We don't think in sentences.
That's why the writer doesn't use proper sentences at the end of passage B.

Continued ▶ ▶ ▶

Your turn!

The stories could be told from a different viewpoint. Here are some possibilities.

Now continue one of the stories from a different viewpoint.

● Choose one of the possibilities above or introduce a new character if you want.
● Choose either to write in the first person (I …) or the third person (He/She …).

Whatever you decide, it must be from one character's viewpoint only.

Write at least another six sentences. Build up to a good ending. Use the frame on the opposite page if you wish.

There I was, lying in the cave when

I looked up and

So I

Suddenly

Improving your work

3.4

Working with a partner, read each other's work and re-check these points.

- Have you stuck to one person's viewpoint?
- Is it clear whose viewpoint you have used?

Summary

- Narrative viewpoint means through whose eyes a story is told (see page 17).
- Sentences can be active or passive. They have different effects (see page 14).
- First person narrative uses 'I' and 'me'; third person uses 'he/she' and 'him/her' (see page 17).

A4 Two views of battle

A4 Two views of battle

Let's investigate...

- How can writers express personal values in an account?
- How can writers express their feelings on a subject?

Objectives	
Word	1
Sentence	3, 5
Reading	1, 6, 7
Writing	5, 6
Speaking/Listening	

▶ Starting points: homophones

Remember:

A homophone is a word that sounds the same, or very similar, to another word, but which is spelled differently and has a different meaning. For example, *board/bored*.

BEWARE! Computer spellchecks don't catch homophone mistakes.

Homophone mistakes rarely lead to the reader misunderstanding the passage. This is because the context (the words around the mistake) usually help the reader to know what the writer really meant.

However, these misspellings can be irritating to the reader who knows the correct homophone, and in test situations you will lose marks in some cases.

Look out for a homophone in the first sentence of extract 1.

4.1

Choose the correct homophone in each sentence. Use a dictionary if you need to.

- Can you give me some *advise/advice*?
- What *affect/effect* will the medicine have?
- I'm doing a *coarse/course* in how to be *coarse/course*.
- He had a *quiet/quite* smile (not really a homophone, but often misused for the same reason).
- I'm *to/too/two* full *to/too/two* eat *to/too/two* puddings.

Reading: comparing two views of battle

Extract 1

Native American medicine man Black Elk remembers fighting at the Battle of Little Big Horn – 'Custer's Last Stand' in 1876. He was 13 at the time.

Soon the soldiers were all crowded into the river, and many Lakotas too; and I was in the water awhile. Men and horses were all mixed up and fighting in the water, and it was like hail falling in the river. Then we were out of the river, and people were stripping dead soldiers and putting the clothes on themselves. There was a soldier on the ground and he was still kicking. A Lakota rode up and said to me: 'Boy, get off and scalp him.' I got off and started to do it. He had short hair and my knife was not very sharp; He ground his teeth. Then I shot him in the forehead and got his scalp.

Chief Sitting Bull, leader of the Sioux at Little Big Horn.

Many of our warriors were following the soldiers up a hill on the other side of the river. Everybody else was turning back downstream, and on a hill away down yonder above the Santee camp there was a big dust, and our warriors whirling around in and out of it just like swallows, and many guns were going off.

I thought I would show my mother my scalp, so I rode over towards the hill where there was a crowd of women and children. ...

When I got to the women on the hill they were all singing and making the tremolo to cheer the men fighting across the river in the dust on the hill. My mother gave a big tremolo just for me when she saw my first scalp.

ed. John Neihardt, *Black Elk Speaks*

Continued ▶ ▶ ▶

Extract 2

Mary Seacole was a Jamaican nurse who attended soldiers during the Crimean War (1853–6). She describes the end of a battle.

It was a fearful scene; but why repeat this remark. All death is trying to witness – even that of the good man who lays down his life hopefully and peacefully; but on the battlefield, when the poor body is torn and rent in hideous ways, and the scared spirit struggles to loose itself from the still strong frame that holds it tightly to the last, death is fearful indeed. It had come peacefully enough to some. They lay with half-opened eyes, and a quiet smile about the lips that showed their end to have been painless; others it had arrested in the heat of passion, and frozen on their pallid faces a glare of hatred and defiance that made your warm blood run cold. But little time had we to think of the dead, whose business it was to see after the dying, who might yet be saved. The ground was thickly cumbered with the wounded, some of them calm and resigned, others impatient and restless, a few filling the air with their cries of pain – all wanting water, and grateful to those who administered it, and more substantial comforts. You might see officers and strangers, visitors to the camp, riding about the field on this errand of mercy. And this, although surely it could not have been intentional – Russian guns still played upon the scene of action. There were many others there, bent on a more selfish task. The plunderers were busy everywhere. It was marvellous to see how eagerly the French stripped the dead of what was valuable, not always, in their brutal work, paying much regard to the presence of a lady.

ed. Alexander and Dewjee, *The Wonderful Adventures of Mrs Seacole*

▷ Reading focus: have you understood?

4.2

Discuss the questions below with a partner. Then write your answers on your own.

- How would you describe, in one simple sentence, the basic story we are told in extracts 1 and 2.

  For example:

  In extract 1, a Native American describes how . . .

- What things are similar in the two accounts?
- How would you feel being in the position of Mary Seacole or Black Elk?
- Compare Black Elk's attitude to battle with Mary Seacole's.
- Find the two images (word pictures) Black Elk uses for the fighting men.
- What two different types of death does Mary Seacole describe?

▷ Writing: modelling how it's done

The two extracts show two different writing approaches, as this table explains. Check through to make sure you can find these examples. Pinpoint them with your finger.

Black Elk's story	Mary Seacole's story
Tells his own personal story – what he did, and a particular incident (the scalping).	Describes a particular battle – but little about what she did. No one person picked out.
Describes events in the order in which they took place.	Gives no clear sequence of events; just describes a scene and lots of different images.
Makes no comment on battles in general.	Comments on battlefields generally.
Gives strong images of what the scene looked like.	Provides strong visual images.
Does not tell us directly what he feels, but the passage implies he is proud.	Tells us directly what she feels.

Continued ▶ ▶ ▶

Your turn!

Plan an account of a crowded scene by copying and completing this writing frame.
You could write about a battle, but the pictures below suggest other possible options.

Describe who you are/your part in the scene.	I am the host of the party …
Include one incident in detail – as when Black Elk describes taking his first scalp.	A girl spills a dark coloured drink over my dad's best coat …
Include one comment showing your feelings about the scene – like Mary Seacole.	I felt the blood drain from my cheeks. Now I could never keep the party a secret …
Include one image to help the reader to picture the scene (when Black Elk says the warriors are 'just like swallows', this is an image).	The queue for the toilet was like a slowly-moving drunken snake …
Think of other details you could add.	My mum's cat stuck on the roof … The old neighbour knocking on our door asking if she could join in … A family photo hanging at an angle about to fall … The smell of something burning, or burnt … A packet of crisps emptied into my sister's pillow case …

Improving your work

4.4

- Have you included details that will help readers to imagine the scene?
- Are there any other details appealing to the senses that you could add?
- See the ICT Zone below for more help on improving your writing.

ICT Zone: spellchecking and improving sentences

4.5

Write a paragraph using the homophones given at the start of this unit, and any others you can think of. Then copy it, replacing the homophones with the wrong spellings. See whether your computer spellchecker picks up the mistakes.

4.6

Type up your story from your plan into a word processing document, and then highlight with a different colour some, or all of, the nouns and verbs in the passage, like this:

> Someone was moving slowly in the room to the music coming from the CD player.

Now try to find more specific, or more powerful words. You can add adverbs or adjectives to help improve the description.

> A small teenage girl was swaying drunkenly in the lounge to the vibrating rhythm booming from the CD player.

Summary

- Homophones are words that sound the same but mean different things (see page 20).
- When writing an account, you can simply describe events as they happened, or comment on them as well (see page 23).
- Images can make it easier for a reader to picture what you describe (see page 24).
- Improve your sentences by using more powerful nouns and verbs, and adding adverbs and adjectives (see page 25).

A5 Phantom focus ▶ ▶ ▶

 A5 Phantom focus

Let's investigate...

- How do writers capture our interest?
- How can non-fiction entertain and present emotions?

Objectives	
Word	7
Sentence	7
Reading	8
Writing	5, 7
Speaking/Listening	

▶ Starting points: reading between the lines

Good writing is not always completely straightforward.
Sometimes you have to 'read between the lines' for the hidden meaning.

5.1

What is the hidden meaning in these sentences?

For example, does the superstar description suggest the reporters were like irritating flies?

The superstar swatted away the reporters.

My husband's just driving his new toy round the block.

My wallet seems to have wandered into your pocket.

My confidence faltered a little as the rogue elephant charged.

The boss made him an offer he couldn't refuse.

The following extract will require you to 'read between the lines'. It is the start of a non-fiction feature published at Halloween.

FROLICS WITH PHANTOMS

It was the towels that finally shattered my nerve. Up until then things had been going remarkably well.

I'd shrugged off tales of suicide and violent strangulation with hardly a shiver, and laughed heartily at accounts of doors locking on their own. I'd been thrilled by the stories of ghostly children playing in the dining room, and intrigued by reports of a freezing 'supernatural mist' by the front door.

I'd even managed a wan smile when co-owner John Langley told me he'd found a mound of human bones – dating from the Great Plague – under the dining room floorboards, and lifted one up to find it was a forearm connected to a skeletal human hand.

Admittedly, my confidence had faltered a little when Sarah, an ex-chambermaid I met in the bar, told me that she wouldn't sleep in the room I was in 'for a million pounds'. Her sister Amanda worryingly concurred, adding that she 'wouldn't sleep in there for all the money in the world'.

It was at this point that I questioned whether my fee from *The Big Issue* was big enough. The towels convinced me that it wasn't.

The facts are these: when I'd left my room at 8pm to go down to the bar, my towels were neatly stacked on top of my chest of drawers; when I returned at closing time, they were sprawled untidily across my bed.

Now this may not seem particularly scary if you're reading this on the bus or in a well-lit bar. But let me assure you that in a creepy, shadowy room, in a rambling fourteenth-century inn, with a long, dark night ahead of you, it was pretty damn close to terrifying.

I searched desperately for a rational explanation. Perhaps I'd thrown the towels onto the bed myself and forgotten about it?

But I knew I hadn't. Perhaps someone had entered my room and moved them? It was possible ... but unlikely. Not least because I'd spent the evening gabbing with the principal suspects.

There was clearly only one explanation: a horrible, salivating ghoul had manifested itself in my room, picked up my towels and chucked them violently onto my bed. I felt sick. It was going to be a long night.

Neil del Strother,
The Big Issue 461

Reading focus: have you understood?

5.2

Talk about the questions below with a partner. Then write your answers on your own.

- How does the title suggest what kind of feature this will be?
- At what point does the writer start to lose confidence?
- Find at least one place where the writer is joking.
- How does the opening of the feature grab our interest?

 # Writing: modelling how it's done

The opening paragraph makes us wonder how the writer's nerve could be shattered by something as ordinary as a pile of towels. It also sets a fairly jokey tone.

His style
- He considers how the messy towels could be explained.
- He half-jokes about *'a horrible, salivating ghoul'*.
- He is really joking about the fears he had at the time – though he is exaggerating them.
- To appreciate the joke you have to 'read between the lines'.
- Finally, he prepares us for more: *'It was going to be a long night.'*

5.3

Your turn!

Write the beginning of a magazine feature about ghosts.

Use the writing frame to help you.

Paragraph 1	It was the _____ (give a detail – like the towels in the extract) that finally shattered my nerve. Up until then _____ (describe how things were before this event).
Paragraph 2	Admittedly, my confidence had faltered a little when _____ (give a slightly worrying detail).
Paragraph 3	It was at this point that I _____ (describe how you felt).
Paragraph 4	The facts are these: _____ (explain what happened).
Paragraph 5	There was only one explanation: _____ (give it: you could exaggerate to make it funny).

Summary

- You may have to 'read between the lines' for hidden meanings in texts (see page 26).
- One way to start an account is to raise questions and keep the reader guessing (see page 28).
- You can build up to a climax within a piece of writing (see page 28).

Literary Fiction and Non-fiction Profile (Units 1–5)

1. Reading

The main extracts I read were:
- Ernest Shackleton, *South*
- Neil Arksey, *MacB*
- David Almond, *Kit's Wilderness*
- Gary Paulsen, *The Fourteenth Summer*
- John Neidhart (ed.), *Black Elk Speaks*
- Alexander and Dewjee (ed.), *The Wonderful Adventures of Mrs Seacole*
- Neil del Strother, *Frolics with Phantoms*

2. Writing

In this section I have:
- made notes on literary description
- written an action-packed account with a build-up
- continued a story from a different viewpoint
- planned an account of a crowd scene
- written the beginning of a magazine feature about ghosts.

3. Key learning

I have learned how to:
- use formal and informal English
- use active and passive sentences
- speed up an account with short sentences
- spot homophones (same sound, different meanings)
- build up to a climax
- 'read between the lines' for hidden meanings
- use different narrative viewpoints
- describe and comment on events
- use images in a description
- raise questions to keep the reader guessing.

4. Extension

I completed the following Challenge tasks:
- spotting connections
- ICT: spellchecking and improving sentences.

B1 Introduction

Let's investigate...

- Can you trust factual writing?

Objectives	
Word	
Sentence	7
Reading	8, 11
Writing	4, 6, 13
Speaking/Listening	

▶ Starting points: factual writing

Remember...

- Non-literary non-fiction writing is usually thought of as factual writing. Normally, we might think of

reports

information texts (such as encyclopaedias)

instructions

But, as you will have seen in your work in school, many texts aren't just reports, or just information texts.

- **Many of these give you facts, but they only give you some facts, and ignore others.**

- **They use powerful or clever language, which is actually quite persuasive.**

The labels on food and drink packaging are examples of texts that give some facts but not others.
By law these products must provide certain information about what ingredients are in them. However, is that all they provide?

Look at the following example.

QUENCH!

pure natural water

Do you:

- feel sluggish?
- get headaches?
- yawn constantly?
- forget things?
- lose track of a conversation?

In that case, you probably aren't drinking enough water:

TRY QUENCH!

FACT: Lack of water is the #1 trigger of daytime fatigue.

FACT: A mere 2% drop in your body water can trigger fuzzy short-term memory, trouble with basic maths and difficulty focusing on the computer screen or on a printed page.

FACT: You need 6–8 glasses of water a day to remain healthy.

QUENCH!

is water collected from a natural bubbling spring in the heart of Wales.

6 94327 0054 .978

Best before: see bottle lid

Keep cool and store in a clear dry place.

Typical analysis is per litre: calcium 12mg, magnesium 8mg, sodium 11mg, potassium 5mg, nitrates 6mg, chlorides 13mg, sulphates 8mg, silica 31mg.

Reading focus: have you understood?

1.1

Discuss the following questions with your group.

- What product is this a label for?
- What impression of water is the label/text trying to give?
- Decide on five words to describe the tone of the text. (Does it create a dull, heavy mood, or something else?) Try to use words other groups might not think of.
- How is the factual information made to seem serious?
- What effect does the use of the word 'you' have?

Writing: modelling how it's done

As you can see, there is much more to this text than just factual information.

Consider this sentence:

> Fact: a mere 2% drop in your body water can trigger fuzzy short-term memory, trouble with basic maths and difficulty focusing on the computer screen or on a printed page.

Is this a fact? The use of the word 'can' means that the advertisers are playing safe. It 'can' seriously affect you, but it might not!

1.2

Your turn!

Make up a new style label for a new toothbrush.

Try to make your product sound
fun, exciting and essential.

Use some of these 'made up' facts, if you wish.
They are in note form so you will have to turn them into short, but punchy, sentences or phrases.

- Regular brushing of teeth can stop tooth decay.

- 80% of users said they felt fresher after use.

- Cleaner teeth make a fresher smile.

1.3

Explaining my ideas

Start by copying and completing this writing frame to explain how you designed your new product label.

I designed a new label for _____ .

I wanted to give my product a _____ image so I chose to use _____ colours. These _____ make it seem _____ .

The main focus of the text is _____ . I decided to make this my focus to suggest to the customer the product is _____ .

Other features I included are _____ . I included these because I wanted to _____ .

Overall I am _____ with my label as I think it _____ .

Looking ahead

Like the work you have just done, this section looks at how non-literary non-fiction texts work. In particular:

• How the choice of language can influence the reader.
• How the structure can add power.
• How the layout and presentation can add impact.

Summary

• Facts can be used persuasively (see page 30).
• Factual information can be presented in an interesting way (see page 31).
• Using numbers or percentages can give a writer authority (see page 31).

B2 Loaded language

Let's investigate...

- How can informative letters also persuade?
- How do you write 'loaded' language?

Objectives	
Word	7
Sentence	7, 9
Reading	8, 12
Writing	6, 12, 13, 14
Speaking/Listening	

▶ Starting points: loaded language

Read these two texts. They both come from wildlife documentaries about the life of stray cats.

Shivering in the cold, damp darkness, the fragile mother cat hesitates before jumping on the soft scuttling sound she hears. With relief she finds she has caught a mouse; tonight her children will have some food to keep them alive.

Crouched, ready to pounce under the cloak of dark, the warrior female cat pounces on the scuttling sound her keen ears have located. With a sense of satisfaction she finds she has snared another mouse; tonight her tribe will have a feast.

Essentially, the same events happen in each piece, but the impression is quite different.

2.1

Read the two texts again, and try each of these activities.

- Choose a simple title for each of the two documentaries. The titles should show the differences in the film-maker's attitude.

  You might want to select from this list.

  Stray Cat Blues

  Hunter on the Streets

  Cat Attack

  Cats Under Threat

  Feline Feelings

  Survival of the Fittest

- Draw a very quick sketch of each cat, based on the two descriptions on page 34.

- Finally, make two lists of key words or phrases used to describe the two cats. For example:

  Cat 1

  shivering
  damp
  darkness

  Cat 2

  crouched
  cloak of dark

The words you have picked are the 'loaded' words that make us react in a certain way. For example, 'cat' is just a description, but the words 'warrior' and 'mother' make us think about the cat in a particular way.
Now read the following text. It is full of loaded language.

Reading: information letter ▶ ▶ ▶

Reading: information letter

'Food store of
the year 2004'

Faster Food Xpress,
PO Box 321, London.

Dear Householder,

I am writing to inform you that your house is to be removed, in order to make way for a fantastic new Faster Food Xpress.

Faster Food Xpress outlets are desperately needed in your area and we strive to satisfy our customers. To this end we are going to build a new Faster Food Xpress to match demand. Unfortunately, your house is in the way of our chosen location and we have obtained planning permission to remove it. Obviously, you will be fully compensated and can choose a new house from a range of very desirable properties.

A special advisor, Mrs Catherine Chapman, has been appointed to help you through every step of the way. Naturally, we care about you and your family. Catherine's task is to be on hand as you need her. She will contact you within the week to help you with the exciting task of choosing your dream home.

We sincerely regret any distress this process might cause, and will do everything in our power to help with your move. We are sure you will agree, however, that the benefits for the community as a whole will make your inconvenience worthwhile.

Yours,

James Dinning

James Dinning
Director, Faster Food Xpress

Reading focus: have you understood?

2.2

Discuss these questions with one other person, then answer them in full sentences.

- The word 'removed' is used to say what is going to happen to the house. Think of three alternative, stronger words that might have been used.
- The property is referred to as a 'house', but the alternative accommodation offered is called a 'home'. What is the difference between these two words?
- Why do you think these terms have been used?
- Why is the special advisor called by her first name once she has been introduced?
- What would your response be if you received a letter like this? Why?

Writing: modelling how it's done

Although a letter like this might never be sent, it is a useful example of an information letter. Let's look at how it works:

1. It keeps things simple

- It is short and clear.
- It sets out the situation and informs us what is going to happen.
- Each paragraph deals with a new part of the situation.
- But, it doesn't just tell us the house is going to be knocked down.

2. It uses loaded language

- It uses positive descriptions; 'fantastic new' and 'desperately needed'.
- It uses positive verbs; 'we strive', 'we care' and 'we sincerely regret'.
- It uses neutral, simple descriptions instead of unpleasant ones ('removed' rather than 'demolished').

3. It makes a personal connection

- The letter starts with 'I', making a personal statement to begin with.
- The company is 'we' – this sounds friendlier and as if a group are sharing the responsibility.
- It uses 'you', which is very personal and direct.
- The special advisor is introduced in full, and then her first name 'Catherine' is used.

4. It balances the negative

- Bad things are matched with good things to make the bad news bearable.
- The house has to be removed, but it's all in a good cause; '… to make way for a fantastic new Faster Food Xpress'.
- You will suffer 'inconvenience', but everyone else will benefit.

Continued ▶ ▶ ▶

2.3 *f*

Your turn!

Write a draft letter to the council.
Persuade them not to let Faster Food Xpress knock your house down.

Use some of the techniques James Dinning did, numbered 1–4 on page 37.

Remember the model:

Make a personal connection

Use loaded language

Balance the negative

Keep it simple and clear

Use **this** frame, if you wish.

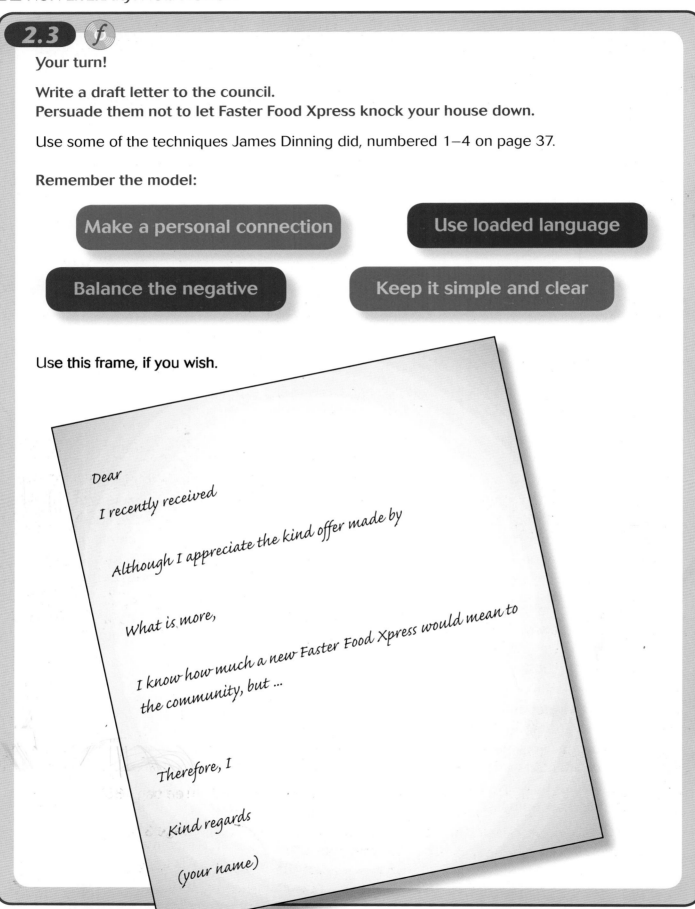

Dear

I recently received

Although I appreciate the kind offer made by

What is more,

I know how much a new Faster Food Xpress would mean to the community, but ...

Therefore, I

Kind regards

(your name)

Improving your work

2.4

Once you have finished your draft letter, go through and improve it, adding these extra techniques.

1. 'Butter them up'
Make your councillor feel really important and knowledgeable. Use phrases such as:
- *I know you must be aware of the dangers of …*
- *You are the only person who …*
- *You have worked so hard to improve our environment, it would be such a shame if …*

2. Use experts
Use evidence, especially when supported by the name of the expert, to strengthen your argument.
- *Experts have shown a disturbing link between junk food and …*
- *Doctors have proved stress levels can become dangerous if …*
- *Psychologists suggest the community spirit of a town can be destroyed if …*

3. Use rhetorical questions
- *Can we really allow this company to destroy our beloved town?*
- *Should we just sit down and accept everything they decide?*
- *Will more litter really improve our community?*

ICT Zone

2.5

Produce a poster, using a DTP program or Word, to inform people of a meeting about James Dinning's plans. Include:

- a slogan to catch their attention (this will probably show your bias!)
- details of the venue, date and time
- some details to explain why people should attend
- eye-catching images
- careful use of colour.

SAY NO TO FASTER FOOD XPRESS!!!

Summary

- Find exactly the right word for the effect you want (use a thesaurus) (see page 35).
- Include a personal touch when trying to persuade (see page 37).
- A good business letter tends to be short, clear and to the point (see page 37).
- Persuade by complimenting your reader (see page 39).
- Refer to expert opinion to make your argument seem stronger (see page 39).
- Add weight to your argument by using rhetorical questions (see page 39).

B3 Spot check ▶ ▶ ▶

Let's investigate...

- How can you make an information and explanation text easier to read?
- How can you analyse and explain how a text works?

Objectives	
Word	4
Sentence	4, 6
Reading	1, 8, 12
Writing	3, 4, 16, 17
Speaking/Listening	

▶ Starting points: using evidence

If you want people to take your ideas seriously you have to use evidence to support them.

Sam: Manchester United's the best team ever.
Donna: You're always saying that. It's getting boring.
Sam: Well, they won the treble in 1999, and they were the first English team to win the European Cup, and …
Donna: OK, OK, it's all right, you've made your point!

Without his evidence, Sam's statement meant nothing.

Question: How do you provide evidence in a school essay?
Answer: Follow three steps for each paragraph:

> 1. Make your point.
> 2. Give evidence or provide an example in your own words.
> 3. Explain it in as much detail as possible.

Here is what one student wrote about the label in the last unit.

	We are persuaded to buy Quench! *because the advertisers make us worry about lack of water. For example, the label states 'lack of water is the number one trigger of daytime fatigue'.*

Now read this information text.

▶ Reading: information text

Help! I've got spots!

Don't panic. They don't mean you are dirty or have been pigging out on too much choccy. They just show that your body is changing. Over 80% of teenagers suffer from spots at some point so you're not weird.

Major acne triggers:

1. exams
2. stress
3. new relationship
4. before a period
5. tensions at home
6. some cosmetics
7. some medicines
8. relationship breaking up
9. puberty

What are they anyway?

Spots are called acne by doctors (this word comes from the Greek word 'acme' meaning 'the prime of life' – bit of a joke, eh?)

Acne is just oily skin with lumps. Sounds simple but it's not and it can be really frustrating and upsetting.

How come I've got them?

Acne occurs in places where we have sebaceous glands. These are found at the bottom of the tiny hair follicles we have on our face, back and chest.

Puberty or a major event (see box) can set acne off. This is what happens:

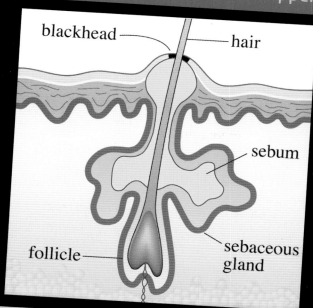

1. Trigger (puberty or event such as stress or exams).
2. The glands go crazy and produce too much sebum (oil).
3. This oil sticks to dead skin cells and blocks the hair follicle.
4. A whitehead forms. If this pushes through the skin it turns black and you've got a blackhead.
5. The spot might inflame due to bacteria having a party with the sebum and dead skin cells. This is when it gets red, angry and really big. It grows until you've a giant custardy top ready for the big squeeze.

41

Continued ▶ ▶ ▶

What can I do about them?

Look after yourself and your skin.

- Wash the skin with water and a mild cleanser twice a day. There are lots of products – use the mildest one possible (strong ones can dry your skin out).
- Drink lots of water and moisturise your skin to keep it healthy.
- Eat a balanced diet – plenty of fruit and veg.
- Get fresh air and exercise whenever possible – but if it's sunny use sunblock!
- If it gets really bad, talk to your pharmacist or doctor. Remember, they probably had spots as well!

Can I squeeze?

- ▶ It's red and angry – **DON'T TOUCH IT!**
- ▶ It's yellow – **GO FOR IT!**
  - Wash your hands – you don't want to get it infected.
  - Put a tissue over your fingers – you don't want the pus on the mirror.
  - Squeeze with your fingers, not your nails.
  - Enjoy!
  - Dab the spot with antiseptic and wash your hands.
  - Leave it well alone now, you don't want it to scar, do you?

- ▶ It's a whitehead – **DON'T TOUCH IT!**
- ▶ It's a blackhead – **GO FOR IT!** Follow the instructions for the yellow ones.

▶ Reading focus: have you understood?

3.1

With a friend, discuss and answer the following questions.

- What percentage of teenagers suffers from spots at some point?
- What is acne?
- Name at least three major triggers of acne.
- Which spots can you squeeze?
- Why does the text use questions as sub-headings?
- Who is meant to read this text? How can you tell?

Writing: modelling how it's done

This is an information and explanation text for teenagers.
It is about a sensitive subject so uses some clever tricks to tell the reader about spots without sounding like a boring parent.

1. It's on the level

It's like having a chat with a mate; it uses the first person for the sub-heading questions and the second person to answer.
- 'What can I do about them?'
- 'You need to look after yourself and your skin.'

2. It's a friendly expert

It mixes informal language with technical and scientific language.
This way is sounds as if it knows what it is talking about.
- 'choccy'
- 'giant custardy top ready for the big squeeze'
- 'this word comes from the Greek word 'acme' meaning 'the prime of life''
- 'Acne occurs in places where we have sebaceous glands.'

3. It's clear and simple

Note the use of:
- sub-headings
- bullet points
- numbered lists
- boxed information.

4. It has an attractive layout

- Use of colour is appealing.
- Technical illustrations are informative and show how spots form.
- Light-hearted illustrations make the leaflet seem friendlier.
- Illustrations of teens with spots show you're not alone.

Continued ▶ ▶ ▶

3.2 *f*

Your turn!

Now, explain how this text works. Use:

- the ideas from the modelling section on page 43.
- the writing frame below.

Copy and complete the frame.

- Follow each starter sentence with evidence (a quote or two) and then explain how these ideas work.
- Remember to use quotation marks around any extracts from the text.
- The more detailed your explanation, the more marks you will get.

The text 'Help, I've got spots!' is written for a ——————— audience and intends

to ——————— ——————————————————————— and tells teenagers

——————————————————————————————— . It has a

why ———————— and how ————————————————————

——————— tone but shows it can be trusted by using ———————

The structure is ————————— **and** ————————— to follow. Finally, the layout and

illustrations are ———————————————————————————— .

The text is like a conversation between two friends, ——————————— .

It mixes informal language with scientific and technical terms ———————— .

It follows a logical structure and makes use of ——————————————— .

The layout and illustrations help the reader ———————— .

In conclusion, this is a successful information and explanation text because

——————————— .

Spelling zone

The 'sh' sound is one of the more difficult ones to remember when spelling words. In the article, there are at least two examples:

relationship   and   *sebaceous*

The 'c' here is like the 'c' in **delicious**, although the ending is different.

There are also spellings with very similar sounds, for example – **moisturise** which has the 'ch' sound before the 't'.

3.3

Copy and underline the part of the word making the 'sh' sound in these words.

smashing

vicious

cautious

anxious

fresh

luscious

Summary

- Provide evidence for your ideas when talking or writing (see page 40).
- Put actual words from the text in quotation marks (see page 44).
- Develop your explanation as fully as possible (see page 44).
- Information and explanation texts can be made personal by using questions (see page 43).
- Mix informal expressions and technical terms to give authority (see page 43).
- The use of sub-headings, bullet points, numbered lists, boxed information and illustrations make information texts easier to read and understand (see page 43).

B4 What do you think? ▷ ▷ ▷

Let's investigate...

- How can you discuss a topic effectively?
- How do you write a discursive essay?

Objectives	
Word	8
Sentence	6, 9
Reading	
Writing	3, 9, 13, 14
Speaking/Listening	

▶ Starting points: revising connectives

Read these sentences.

> I had cheese after my evening meal. I had nightmares.

With these two sentences we cannot tell for certain if eating the cheese caused the nightmares.
Using a connective would help us to understand the intended meaning.

> I had cheese after my evening meal **and** had nightmares.
>
> I had cheese after my evening meal; **consequently** I had nightmares.
>
> I had cheese after my evening meal; **as a result** I had nightmares.

The connectives **and**, **consequently**, and **as a result** have all been used to join the two simple sentences. This makes a compound sentence. However, you may also remember that connectives don't just have to go in the middle of a sentence:

> **Because** I had cheese after my evening meal, I had nightmares.

4.1

Write out new versions of the sentences below using connectives.
Use the box of connectives to help you.

- Kerry decided not to go to the disco. She didn't like the music. Louise wasn't going.
- The film was rubbish. It had no plot. The soundtrack was good. I enjoyed it.
- Alex couldn't watch the match. They were struggling. They should never have fielded that team.

nonetheless	meanwhile	therefore	still	in fact	in any case
consequently	next	as a result	though	for example	incidentally
furthermore	then	however	after all	namely	by the way
later	so	on the other hand	I mean	as well	as
also	either	too	first(ly)	second(ly)	because
finally	besides	equally	similarly	otherwise	
rather	alternatively	in other words	anyway	in the first place	

Reading: discussion

Kate: So, how are we going to get some money?
Jo: I dunno.
Kate: Come on, you must have some ideas.
Jo: Of course I've got ideas.
Kate: Well?
Jo: Well what?
Kate: What are those ideas?
Jo: What ideas?
Kate: Your ideas.
Jo: What about my ideas?
Kate: What are your ideas?
Jo: You want me to tell you my ideas? About what?
Kate: About how we can make some money.
Jo: Oh.
Kate: So ...?
Jo: No, sorry, I haven't got any ideas about that. Hey, what do you call a deer without any eyes?
Kate: No idea.
Jo: Oh, you knew it.

Reading focus: have you understood?

This discussion isn't very successful.
In fact Kate and Jo don't manage to discuss the topic of how to get some money at all.

4.2

Discuss and answer these questions with another person.
● Do Kate and Jo come up with any ideas for getting some money?
● Jo is telling the truth when she says 'Of course I've got ideas'. How can this be?
● Jo is not focused on the topic. What does she do that shows us this?
● What parts of the discussion are linked to the topic of getting some money?

Writing: modelling how it's done

Kate and Jo's discussion doesn't work because it isn't focused.
Jo goes off the topic straight away and they don't manage to decide anything.

Discursive writing or speaking is when you discuss an issue or topic.

To be successful you need to:
● keep your focus
● cover as many relevant points as possible
● provide an answer.

For example, if Kate had been writing about her thoughts, she might have wanted to write about ...

● Whether earning money is a good idea when you are a teenager
● How people pay very little
● Fitting work around school and other activities
● What parents think
● Saving money
● Unsuitable jobs
● Interviews
● Job letters

Her essay might begin like this:

Introduces the topic
(earning money)

Earning money when you are a teenager is
a difficult business. Firstly, nobody wants
to pay you anything at all; they think – 'oh,
here's a teenager, she must be stupid, she'll be
happy with a fizzy drink and a sponge cake as
payment.' So, how do you do deal with this?

Covers the first point
(how people won't
pay much)

Moves on to the next
point (how to deal
with this problem)

Other paragraphs could deal with each
of Kate's ideas or points in turn.

She could end by summing up her ideas.

As you can see, earning money is not at all simple. On
the one hand, you get cash in your pocket, the chance
to buy the clothes you want, and the chance to have a
bit of independence. But weighed against that is the
problem of stingy employers, grumpy parents, lost free
time, and teachers moaning about homework. In fact,
it's probably not worth the bother. Be poor, but happy.

Continued ▶ ▶ ▶

4.3

Now write your own essay to discuss the following topic:

Should children be able to leave school at fourteen?
Follow these steps:

1. Plan by brainstorming ideas for and against this idea.

You must discuss both sides of the argument, as this will make your views seem more reasonable and thoughtful. This has been done for you.

> **FOR**
>
> - *some children not suited to school life*
> - *better than being excluded*
> - *help those who want to stay and learn*
> - *can start learning a trade earlier*
> - *grow up quicker*
>
> **AGAINST**
>
> - *school is for everyone*
> - *too many children on streets already*
> - *no skills or exam means a poor job*
> - *school can offer trades and practical things*
> - *not good to grow up too quickly*

2. Look at your ideas carefully.

Decide what answer you are going to give, and why.

3. Sequence your ideas.

Number the ideas in the brainstorm and put them in an order that is logical and develops in a way your reader will be able to follow.

4. Write your opening paragraph.

This has been done for you, too.

> *School dominates your life from age five to sixteen. But is it a good thing? Just think what life would be like if you could leave school at fourteen. Freedom, independence, long lie-ins in the morning ... but, no qualifications.*

5. Now write the rest of the essay.

Go through the ideas in the order you have chosen. Use connectives to link them. Make sure you develop each idea with an example and explanation.

> *On one hand the benefits are obvious ...*
> *However, there are also drawbacks ...*

6. Finish off.

Sum up your ideas, and arrive at a conclusion.

> *In conclusion, I feel that ...*
> *Clearly, it can be seen that ...*

ICT Zone ▶ ▶ ▶

ICT Zone

4.4

The Internet is a really useful tool for researching different issues.
Use it to get up-to-date facts to support your side of the discussion.

For example, the government now offers 'Modern Apprenticeships' for school leavers.
These are designed to provide job training for school leavers in key skill areas.
Look at the website **www.realworkrealplay.info** and see how this information could be used in your essay on leaving school at fourteen.

Summary

- Connectives are signals to your reader or listener. They tell them how ideas link (see page 46).
- If a discussion is going to be successful it has to stay on topic (see page 48).
- In discursive essays, cover both sides of the argument to show you have considered things carefully (see page 50).
- Make your essay or speech logical and ensure it develops naturally. Connectives can help to do this (see page 50).
- Write a strong conclusion (see page 51).

Non-literary/Non-fiction Profile (Units 1–4)

1. Reading

The main extracts I read were:
- an information letter
- a spot fact sheet (information)
- a discussion.

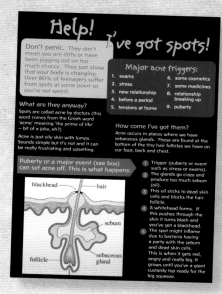

2. Writing

In this section I have:
- written a new style label for a product of my choice
- written a letter to persuade the council not to allow my house to be knocked down
- written an essay analysing how the spot fact sheet works
- written a discursive essay: should children be able to leave school at 14?

3. Key learning

I have learned how to:
- mix fact and fun to create an image
- understand the power of loaded language
- write an information letter
- write a persuasive letter
- write an information and explanation fact sheet
- write an analysis
- use connectives
- write a discursive essay.

4. Extension

I completed the following Challenge tasks:
- a poster using a DTP program to inform people of a meeting
- using the Internet for research to support an essay.

C1 Introduction

Let's investigate...

- How close is poetry to music?

Objectives	
Word	
Sentence	
Reading	6, 16
Writing	4, 5, 8
Speaking/Listening	

▶ **Starting points:** poetry and music

Remember...

Poetry is close to music. The ballad, which is a story in song, is one of the earliest forms of poetry.

- Traditional ballads are written in rhyme, usually in verses of four lines called stanzas (though not every writer keeps to this pattern).
- At one time ballads were passed around by word of mouth so the words would have changed as they went from one person to another. In this way the story developed and the ballad took shape.
- Most ballads contain a message about life.

- Look up the word 'ballad' in a dictionary.
- Where does it come from? How is it related to dance?
- What was its original meaning?

Reading: ballad

Oscar Wilde (1856–1900) wrote a famous ballad called 'The Ballad of Reading Gaol'.

He used a direct simple style suited to the ballad form.
This is the first verse.

He did not wear his scarlet coat,
For blood and wine are red,
And blood and wine were on his hands
When they found him with the dead,
The poor dear woman whom he loved,
And murdered in her bed.

Reading focus: have you understood?

1.2

This verse conjures up a very dramatic scene.

It is written in six lines, not four like most early ballads.
Read lines 1–4 first, then pause.
Now read the remaining two lines.
- Why are these last two lines important?
- How do they make you feel and what extra information are you given?
  Talk with a partner about your ideas.

Continued ▶ ▶ ▶

Reading: ballad

Here are five more verses of 'The Ballad of Reading Gaol'.

Yet each man kills the thing he loves,
By each let this be heard,
Some do it with a bitter look,
Some with a flattering word,
The coward does it with a kiss,
The brave man with a sword!

Some kill their love when they are young,
And some when they are old;
Some strangle with the hands of Lust,
Some with the hands of Gold:
The kindest use a knife, because
The dead so soon grow cold.

Some love too little, some too long,
Some sell, and others buy;
Some do the deed with many tears,
And some without a sigh:
For each man kills the thing he loves,
Yet each man does not die.

He does not die a death of shame
On a day of dark disgrace,
Nor have a noose about his neck,
Nor a cloth upon his face,
Nor drop feet-foremost through the floor
Into an empty space.

Reading focus: have you understood?

1.3

Talk about the verses with a partner. Make sure you understand what the last verse depicts.

Then discuss these questions.

- What view of human love is presented here? Try to sum this up together in a sentence.
- In what different ways is this view acted out?
- Do you agree with the view about love that is expressed?

Try to read the whole of Oscar Wilde's famous ballad.
You could work with a partner, reading a verse at a time.

Looking ahead

In the next section you will have a chance to read another narrative poem, this time a rap.
A rap could be described as a modern-day ballad.
You will also be able to write and perform your own rap poem.

In this chapter you will discover other things about poetry, such as ways of:
- building images
- creating metaphors
- using powerful verbs.

Summary

- Poetry can be close to music, as in ballads (see page 54).
- Ballads tell stories, but also have a message, or 'lesson' for the reader (see page 54).
- Traditional ballads were written in rhyme (see page 54).
- Ballads were usually written in four lines called stanzas (see page 54).
- Some writers changed this pattern to suit what they wanted to say (see page 54).

C2 Rap and rhyme

Let's investigate...

- How can you write a narrative poem?
- What are the important features of a rap?
- What different kinds of rhymes are there? How can you use them?

Objectives	
Word	
Sentence	
Reading	6, 16
Writing	4, 5, 8
Speaking/Listening	

▶ Starting points: rhymes

Poets make rhymes in all sorts of ways. They may use full rhymes such as 'cap' and 'rap' or they may choose words that nearly rhyme.

For example in 'Baseball Cap' on page 59, 'cap' rhymes with 'back'.

2.1

Write down all the words from each line you think could rhyme with the word in green.

track	told	flat	sack	spin	rat	clip	trap
grin	cloud	him	thank	string	well	win	rabbit
cone	comb	make	sail	drone	own	sweet	crumb
chime	dime	rhyme	sound	fold	mine	give	crime

2.2

Double rhymes have two rhymes. 'Michael' rhymes with 'cycle'.

Write down the only word in each line that double rhymes with the word in green.

telling	asking	tapping	reading	selling	ending	singing
label	travel	towel	canal	hospital	handle	table
sulky	sunny	baggy	bulky	sandy	milky	celery

Reading: a rap

Rhythm and rhyme are very important in rap because a rap is a musical narrative poem.

Read the first few lines of this rap, and decide:

- how you would perform it
- what parts you would stress.

Read the rest of 'Baseball Cap' stressing the beat as you go.

Baseball Cap

Uh, smack, there goes my baseball cap!
I'm on the floor, I took-a- took-a bruise to my jaw
Jumped me from behind, at least three, maybe four –
I never see my hat no more.

Oh, smash, there goes my baseball cap
It's gone, gone, gone, gone – I can't get it back.
[Repeat]

Fourteen years old and hard through the core
I'm walking home making plans for war
My hands was cut, my uncle say: 'What's up?
Let me guess, your clothes are in a mess, you're in distress.
Sit down, take five and let me look at your knees
You're still alive, son, please take it easy.
Sometimes you have to let the world know you aren't bluffing,
But enough is enough – don't lose your life over nothing.
Scuffling in the street is no way to die
And I don't want to have to meet your momma's eye.
So try and listen hard before you fall into the trap
Of making war over a baseball cap'.

Oh, smash, there goes my baseball cap
It's gone, gone, gone, gone – I can't get it back.
[Repeat]

59

Continued ▶ ▶ ▶

Reading: continued

I sat back, had a think and Uncle poured a drink
I had a little cry, my eyes started to blink
Cos what occurred from his words to me
Sounds absurd, but I heard the love in his voice for me.
I made a choice, it was like 'snap'
What's that cap when I've got something real like that?
I can measure it, treasure it and at my leisure sit
Down with those who mean the most to me
The baseball cap was a ghost, this is real to me.
'You've got steel, son,' my uncle's talking,
'Takes a champion to walk and keep walking.
Drink your drink, let the words sink in,
say goodnight to your ma and think again'.
So I took my fourteen years to bed
Everything he said taking root in my head.
I shed all my tears and let my fourteen years
Relax.

Oh, smash, there goes my baseball cap
It's gone, gone, gone, gone – I can't get it back.
[Repeat]

Rollo, Maxi Jazz & Sister Bliss (Faithless)

 Reading focus: have you understood?

2.3

Work with a partner. Answer these questions together.

- Where do you think the story takes place?
- How would you feel if someone stole your cap? What would you do?
- What does the boy decide to do at first?
- What advice is he given? By whom?
- What does he learn?
- Would you call this rap a poem or not? Try to reach a point of view together.

> Writing: modelling how it's done

2.4 *f*

Continue working with a partner.

Copy and complete this timeline of the events in 'Baseball Cap'.

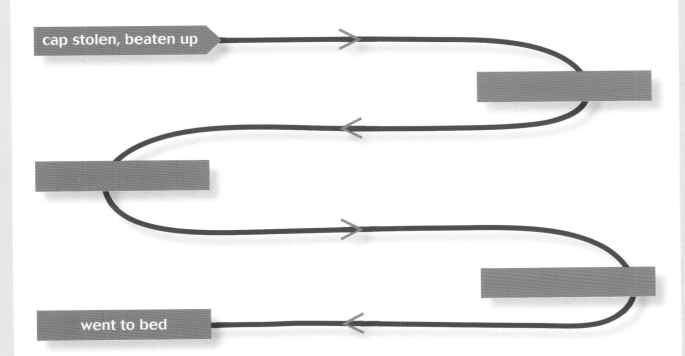

cap stolen, beaten up

went to bed

2.5

With your partner think of a dramatic event or an incident when a possession is stolen or damaged.

Write down a list of four or five ideas like this:

football medals stolen
coin collection stolen
mobile phone stolen

Continued ▶ ▶ ▶

2.6

Baseball Cap' has a chorus. The chorus is two rhyming lines (a couplet) that are repeated:

'Oh, smash, there goes my baseball cap
It's gone, gone, gone, gone – I can't get it back.'

Choose your best dramatic event or incident from 2.5 and write a chorus about it.
Here are some rhymes you could use. Add your own to these.

diamond ring/anything

phone/own

cash/smash

fight/right

Write some couplets. Read the couplets, stressing the beat. Choose the one that works best.

2.7

Read the first four lines of 'Baseball Cap' again. Now write a short verse of your own
with your partner.

> 'Uh, smack, there goes my baseball cap!
> I'm on the floor, I took-a- took-a bruise to my jaw
> Jumped me from behind, at least three, maybe four –
> I never see my hat no more.'

Here are some more rhymes that may give you ideas. Add your own.

distress/mess/ possess/ unless

pain/again/sane/shame/rain/blame

believe/leave/receive

war/core/saw/sore/before

dream/seem/mean/seen

Practise saying your rap together. You could take it in turns to say a line each.

Challenge

2.8

Read all of these instructions before you begin.

Try developing your rap into a longer story. First carry out a brainstorming exercise around the event or object of your rap.
For example:

How did the event happen or possession get stolen?

How did the people involved feel?

BRAINSTORM IDEAS ABOUT ...

Who was involved in the event?

What was the outcome of the event?

Decide roughly what will happen in your story. Remember that you can always change the events as you go. Develop your rap using rhymes. You could:
- use some of the rhymes in 'Baseball Cap', or others in this unit
- add to them
- make up your own rhymes.

2.9

Some lines in 'Baseball Cap' have rhymes in the middle. This stresses the rhythm.
Can you find the middle rhymes in this line?

'I can measure it, treasure it and at my leisure sit'

Find the middle rhymes in the following lines.

**'Down with those who mean the most to me
The baseball cap was a ghost, this is real to me.'**

Try thinking of middle rhymes for your rap.
Learn your rap off by heart and perform it when it is finished.

Summary

- Poetry uses different kinds of rhymes (see page 58).
- A narrative poem tells a story (see page 59).
- A rap is a musical narrative poem (see page 59).
- A poem can have a chorus – lines that are repeated between verses (see page 62).

C3 Writing in lines

C3 Writing in lines

Let's investigate...

- How can you reorder sentences?
- What is a 'line' in poetry? How is it different from a sentence?
- How can you experiment with lines?
- What is free verse?

Objectives	
Word	7
Sentence	1
Reading	
Writing	6, 8
Speaking/Listening	

▶ Starting points: reordering sentences

You can often write the same sentence in different ways.

The car raced along the street **at an unbelievable speed.**

At an unbelievable speed the car raced along the street.

3.1

Write down the sentence above in another way.

Read both sentences stressing 'at an unbelievable speed'. You will see that the pitch of your voice (or cadence) changes with each sentence.

3.2

Finish this sentence.

The paper aeroplane flew in the wind like ...

Then write the sentence in two different orders. Read each one, changing the cadence of your voice. Then, read the poem on page 65.

Reading

Highland Ox

I once knew a beast that roamed
In the Highlands;
Its horns were a truncheon,
Big,
Battered.
The matted hair was an orangutang's chest,
Or a half dried wig
Tossed and strewn about.
Its legs were oak stumps,
The rings showing age,
With a dried crust of mud or bark,
Flaky,
Crumbled.
It had the skin of a rhino
And was tough as leather.
It was wild,
Could have been John the Baptist,
The locusts and honey.
He wandered all day,
But never moved,
Chewing the same cud for years,

Worn white.
Until, one day,
Some men parked a landrover on the brow
of a hill.
One wielded a shot gun.
Suddenly, a crack!
Doves shot out of a nearby forest;
A dog whimpered half a mile away.
And there was a thud
Of rock,
Clay
And heaving bones.
I never saw him again.

Paul Sparkes

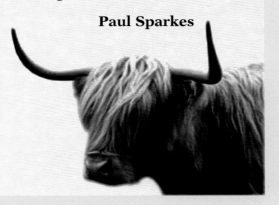

Reading focus: have you understood?

3.3

The poet describes the highland ox as a 'beast'.
- Why does this description suit the animal?
- What features about the ox stand out to you?

John the Baptist was a Jewish preacher who lived at the time of Christ.
He spent several months in the desert without any human contact.
- Why does the poet compare him to the highland ox?

The ox is described in great detail compared with the men who shoot it.
- What impression does this create?

Doves are often used as a symbol of peace.
- Why do you think the poet has chosen to include doves at the end of the poem?

Writing: modelling how it's done ► ► ►

Writing: modelling how it's done

A poem is written in lines, not sentences.

Sometimes a line can be one word.
This occurs in 'Highland Ox'. Here the one-word
lines come after and before a longer line:

'Highland Ox' is a free verse poem. This
means that it has no regular beat or
rhythm repeated throughout the poem.

> I once knew a beast that roamed
> In the Highlands;
> Its horns were a truncheon,
> Big,
> Battered.
> The matted hair was an orangutang's chest,

 3.4

Read these sentences.

> The brown bear rose up, its vast girth, its royal head, its boxer's paws casting immense shadows in the shifting light. Twigs snapped, leaves crunched and tiny creatures scampered as …

Finish the last sentence. Use a thesaurus to find a range of suitable words.

3.5

Here is part of the first
sentence from 3.4, written
in lines.

Read it aloud and think about:
- How the sentence has changed. What words have been cut?
- The punctuation that has been used.
- How the cadence of your voice has changed.
- How a different meaning is conveyed in the last line.

> The brown bear rose up,
> Its vast girth,
> Its royal head,
> Its boxer's paws,
> Immense.
> Shadows in the shifting light.

3.6

Write the sentence that you finished in 3.4 in lines.

- When you have done this try reordering the lines in different ways.
- Replace and cut words.
- Experiment until it sounds the way you want it to.

Challenge

3.7

Write a series of free verse poems (three or four) using the strategies you have learned.

You could write poems about contrasting:
- creatures (such as a deer, a lion, a vulture)
- sport (for example, cycling and darts)
- fruit
- music
- or anything else you prefer.

Complete this free verse poem if you wish. Can you work out what two different sports are being described?

> Polite clapping
> Deafening roars
> Leather hits willow
> Leather hits the net
> One man holds his bat up proudly
> Another man is buried beneath his team-mates
> Hundreds cheer
> Thousands yell

Summary

- A poem is written in lines, not sentences (see page 66).
- Reordering sentences can change the cadence of your voice (see page 66).
- Free verse poetry has no regular beat or rhythm repeated throughout the poem (see page 66).
- Varying the length of lines in a poem creates pace and interest (see page 66).

C4 It's alive!

C4 It's alive!

Let's investigate...

- What is personification?
- What is 'mood'?
- How can you use powerful verbs to create effects?

Objectives	
Word	6, 7
Sentence	
Reading	
Writing	
Speaking/Listening	

▶ Starting points: personification

You may remember that when we give feelings to something that is not human, we 'personify' it. In other words, we make it seem like a person. We often do this in everyday speech. For example we might say that, 'love is blind' or say 'the weather's really playing games with us … '.

4.1

Match the words on the left to those on the right in different ways.

Think about what human strengths or weaknesses would suit each one. For example you might say: 'Spring chatters' or 'Spring startles'.

Then decide which words are the best match.

Write down your choices.

Spring

Summer

Autumn

The sea

Fame

Truth

Power

Knowledge

is greedy

is cruel

chatters

corrupts

forgets

strengthens

sweats

startles

heaves

Reading

Goodnight Stroud

The Clock Tower glowers
Its hands fidget
towards dawn.

Dark streets yawn.
　It's late –
the streets wait –
　restless as rain.

Trains idle up sidelines;
a cyclist sidles by.

Black taxis scuttle
down back alleys.

A bright bus blunders
up the High Street.

The Belisha Beacon blinks.

Parked cars huddle,
like wet toads;
the night thinks
that the stars
are sending morse-code.

Pie Corbett

Reading focus: have you understood?

4.2

Discuss these questions with a partner.

- Stroud is described as though it is human. For example the clock's '*hands fidget*'. Find other examples of personification.
- What time of night is it and what is the weather like?
- Read the first four verses. What kind of mood do you think Stroud is in? Again, think of the streets and other features as human.
- Morse code is a way of sending messages; letters and numbers are sent as signs, using light or sound. Read the last verse. What picture is conjured up in the night sky?

Writing: modelling how it's done

Writing: modelling how it's done

 4.3

There are many powerful verbs in 'Goodnight Stroud' such as *'glowers'* and *'yawn'* in the first and second verses. Find an example in each of the remaining verses.

 4.4

Replace the verbs in bold below with a more powerful one. Use a thesaurus and write down your choices.

> **For example:**
>
> He moans about the weather to his wife.
>   grunts

> He waits at the corner for the boy to appear.

> He drives off, disappearing round the bend.

> She runs along the icy pavement.

> They call goodbye to the boy at the bus-stop.

> The cat follows the night noises.

> She walks confidently across the street to the all-night store.

 4.5

Now use the verbs you have chosen to personify features from a city street, like this:

> The lorry grunts

> The bus-stop loiters

Write them down. Add others to your list. Turn them into a simple poem.

70

Challenge

4.6

Write a longer poem about an urban street scene.

It could be set:

- at night (like 'Goodnight Stroud')
- during a Sunday market (use the image below, if you wish)
- during summer or winter
- when road works are being carried out
- or choose your own setting.

Use your earlier work to develop your ideas; think of the verbs you used in 4.4 and 4.5.

Summary

- Personification is when we give human feelings and characteristics to something that is not human (see page 68).
- Powerful verbs can add impact to a poem (see page 70).
- Mood is the feeling or atmosphere created in a poem (see page 69).

C5 The sixth sense

Let's investigate...

- What is an image?
- How can a poem appeal to the senses?

Objectives	
Word	5, 6, 7
Sentence	
Reading	
Writing	4, 8
Speaking/Listening	

▶ Starting points: imagery

An image in poetry is a picture in the mind that appeals to:

> Sight   Hearing   Smell   Taste   Touch

But when we read a poem the most important experience is how the poem makes us feel. We may feel sadness, happiness, suspense and so on. 'Feeling' is like a sixth sense.

5.1

Read this extract from a poem and talk about the questions in the balloon with a partner.

- What senses does the poem appeal to?

- What feelings does the poem create?

Your small

Brother is making
His balloon squeak like a cat
Seeming to see
A funny pink world he might eat on the other
    Side of it,
He bites,

Then sits
Back, fat jug
Contemplating a world clear as water,
A red
Shred in his little fist.

from 'Balloons' by Sylvia Plath

Reading

Seaside Sonata

(To be sung on the way home.)

a caravan   a travelling man   a razor shell   kiss and tell

a ferry quay   a ruffled sea   knotted wrack   a chalk stack

fish bone   wish bone   high tide   slip'n'slide

kittiwake   waterscape   shore line   strandline

a brittle star   a limpet jar   a muffled bell   a sudden swell

a falling sea

anemone

a melody   a memory

Mary Green

Reading focus: have you understood?

5.2

- What senses does this poem appeal to? Study a line at a time. Check any words you are unsure of in a dictionary.
- What feeling in particular does the poem conjure up?
- The poem is like a chant. What does the rhythm remind you of?
- Where do you think the poem is being chanted? (Think carefully!) How do you know?
- Why is the poem presented the way it is?

Writing: modelling how it's done ▶ ▶ ▶

Writing: modelling how it's done

The poem is also a series of words that you can connect in different ways to build images. The images can then come together, to make a whole scene. In this case, a seascape is created.

5.3

Either choose your own theme (it is best to choose something you know about) or choose a theme from the following:

Antarctica

The Mariana Trench (the deepest trench beneath the ocean)

sailing

a hurricane

mountaineering

a coral island

a rainforest

dancing

Collect and record as many words linked to your chosen theme as you can. You could also make up words.

Here are some words to start you off.

Theme	Words		
Antarctica	ice sheet	wilderness	iceberg
	ice-scape	windswept	ice floe

If you need to, use an encyclopaedia and thesaurus.

5.4

Now choose some of the words relating to your theme. Arrange them into lines.
They do not have to rhyme but they should have a similar rhythm, or beat.
You could also put words together that are linked in other ways.
How do the words in these lines link together apart from the beat?

ice floe icesheet
windswept wilderness

Remember:
Replace words as you need to.
Experiment with the order of words.
Experiment with the rhythm.
Keep reading your poem as you go.
Does it conjure up a picture of your theme?

ICT Zone: poem layout

5.5

Lay out your poem in an interesting way using ICT.

First **key** in your poem.

You could then, for example, **centre your poem** on the page:

Click on your poem and **drag** to highlight.

Click on **centre alignment** (formatting toolbar), like this:

ice floe icesheet
windswept wilderness

How could you use left and right alignment to lay out your poem?

Summary

- Words can create images — pictures in our mind that appeal to our senses (see page 72).
- Building a series of images in a poem will provoke feelings in the reader (see page 74).
- Laying out a poem in different ways can add to its meaning (see page 75).

C6 Swift thunder ▶ ▶ ▶

C6 Swift thunder

Let's investigate...

- What are compound words?
- What are kennings?
- How are kennings similar to metaphors?

Objectives	
Word	4, 5, 6
Sentence	
Reading	15
Writing	4, 8
Speaking/Listening	

▶ Starting points: revising compound words

A compound word is formed by putting two or more words together to make one. This can be done by:

- forming a complete word (eyelash)
- treating two separate words as one (smart card)
- joining words with a hyphen (father-in-law).

6.1

Choose from these words and make up ten new compound words.

horse	phone	yell
shuffle	dragon	worry
hoot	water	mask
space	bait	mouse
cool	hop	storm
club	shadow	screech

6.2

Now choose five compound words from your list and write an unusual dictionary definition for each one. Use hyphens to join them. For example:

> horse-hop *noun* a dance performed by jockeys after winning a race.

76

Reading

The epic poem 'Beowulf' is over a thousand years old, and is the story of a Scandinavian hero and his deeds. It was written in Old English and has been translated into Modern English several times. We do not know who the original poet was.
Read this extract with your teacher.

from **Beowulf**
(the hero Beowulf slays the monster Grendel's mother in this extract.)

He saw among the armour there the sword to bring him victory,
a Giant-sword from former days: formidable were its edges,
a warrior's admiration. This wonder of its kind
was yet so enormous that no other man
would be equal to bearing it in battle-play
– it was a Giant's forge that had fashioned it so well.
The Scylding champion, shaking with war-rage,
caught by its rich hilt, and, careless of his life,
brandished its circles, and brought it down in a fury
to take her full and fairly across the neck,
breaking the bones; the blade sheared
through the death-doomed flesh. She fell to the ground;
the sword was gory; he was glad at the deed.

Anon (translated from Old English by Michael Alexander)

Reading focus: have you understood?

6.3

- What do these words mean?

  formidable   fashioned   hilt   forge   brandished   sheared   gory

  Check your answers in a dictionary.

- What does Beowulf's sword look like?
- Why is it so terrible?
- How would you describe Beowulf?
- How did he kill Grendel's mother?

Writing: modelling how it's done ▶ ▶ ▶

Writing: modelling how it's done

The Anglo-Saxons and Vikings often used *compound* words.

They also created powerful descriptions for their weapons and other possessions.

These compounds are called *kennings*. They describe the character of something.

A *kenning* is a kind of *metaphor* not a *simile*. It does not compare one thing with another using 'like' or 'as'.

Rather, a *kenning* says something *is* something else.

For example a sword could be '*warrior slayer*' or a horse, '*swift thunder*'.

6.4

- Find four compound words in the extract from *Beowulf* and write them down.

6.5

- Think of kennings to replace these words. One example has been done for you.

  Use a thesaurus to help you.

wave-slicer

helmet	spear	oar
shield	horse	sail
warrior	armour	axe
sword	longship	shadow

6.6

Write a description about a warrior viewing the aftermath of a battlefield.
Choose your best kennings (about five) and include them.
You could begin: **He saw before him the battlefield …**

Spelling zone: roots, prefixes and suffixes

You have looked at how compound words are formed. Many words are created by adding prefixes and suffixes to 'roots'. For example:

the root 'fair' + the suffix 'ly' = fairly

the prefix 'un' + the root 'fair' = unfair

6.7

Add the prefixes or suffixes below to the roots to make words. Sometimes you can add more than one prefix or suffix at a time to make a word.

prefixes	roots	suffixes
un aero im	port sense kind judge	ant less ly
non in trans	plane form	ness ing ment

Choose which of the following methods would help you to remember the spellings.

Sounding out each letter   Splitting the word into parts   Trying to remember the whole word

ICT Zone: kennings

ICT Zone: kennings

6.8

- Create a table in Word, like the one below, and paste in clipart of different objects.
- Then, print out and pass the table to a friend to add their own kennings, or complete on screen.
- Alternatively, complete some new kennings for an object or creature, and put them in a table. Then get a friend to search on the web, or on disk, for an appropriate image.

[lion image]	*gazelle-frightener* *fang-sharpener*	[add your own image]	[add kennings]
[add your own image]	[add kennings]	[armchair image]	*bottom-comforter* *sleep-persuader*

Summary

- Compound words are formed by putting two or more words together to make one (see page 76).
- Kennings are compounds that describe the character of something, for example 'warrior slayer' (see page 78).
- You can build up words using prefixes, suffixes and roots (see page 79).

Poetry (Units 1–6)

1. Reading

The main texts I read were:
- *The Ballad of Reading Gaol* by Oscar Wilde
- *Baseball Cap* by Rollo, Maxi Jazz & Sister Bliss
- *Highland Ox* by Paul Sparkes
- *Goodnight Stroud* by Pie Corbett
- *Seaside Sonata* by Mary Green
- from *Beowulf*, translated by Michael Alexander.

2. Writing

In this section I have:
- written a rap
- written free verse
- written a poem with powerful verbs
- written a poem that appeals to the senses
- created kennings
- compiled a kennings chart/table.

3. Key learning

I have learned how to:
- use a range of rhymes
- write a chorus
- define cadence
- define the difference between a sentence and a line
- vary line length
- define personification
- define mood
- define image
- create a metaphor
- create compound words
- understand what prefixes, suffixes and roots are.

4. Extension
I completed the following Challenge tasks:
- developing a rap
- writing a series of additional poems
- developing my use of personification.

MEDIA AND ICT

D1 Introduction

Let's investigate...

- What can you remember about media texts?
- What are the key elements of media texts?

Objectives	
Word	
Sentence	
Reading	10
Writing	4, 12
Speaking/Listening	

▶ Starting points: what is the media?

Remember...

The media is a term used to:

- describe organisations

- describe ways of communicating to large groups of people

The media can be used by us in many ways, for example:

- for entertainment
- to find information
- for communication

The media can also use us, in order to influence what we say, think and do.

▶ Looking ahead

In this section you will explore:
- interactive features available with new media
- the power of advertising
- different perspectives on media texts.

To remind yourself of the various elements that make up a media text, look at this advertisement.

Reading focus: have you understood?

1.1

- What three excuses are given to go to the 'amazement park'?
- What word is usually used instead of 'amazement' for a place of this type?
- Who does the advert suggest would enjoy Legoland Windsor?
- What two adjectives are used to show that the feats and special effects of the Jack Stone Stunt Show are really exciting?
- This advert uses vibrant, primary colours. What sort of atmosphere does this help to create?
- The three circles look rather like thought bubbles. What is this supposed to suggest?

1.2

Look through a selection of magazines and newspapers and find at least three different adverts.

For each one fill in an investigation chart like this one.

Name of product	
First impressions **(the first feature you notice about this product)**	
Slogan **What does this suggest about the product? Any word play?**	
Colours **What image do these create?**	YOUR COMMENTS
Picture **What does this suggest about the product?**	
Intended audience **for the advert? How do you know?**	

Writing: modelling how it's done

Through your reading you will have seen that an advert such as this uses:
- words and phrases in clever ways
- strong, carefully chosen images and layout.

Can you do the same?

1.3

Your turn!

Sketch a plan of a poster to advertise a new (made-up) amusement park aimed at teenagers. You can write in the colours you would use. You do not actually have to complete the final poster.

- Plan by listing the attractions you are going to have.
- Decide which attractions to include on your poster.
- Think of a suitable image. Exciting? Funny? Scary?
- Choose some suitable colours to use.
- Now, think of a name and design a logo and slogan.
- Give an interesting heading to your poster.
- Make sure the information and explanation section tells your potential customer all they need to know:
  - Why they should visit your amusement park.
  - How they can find out more about it.

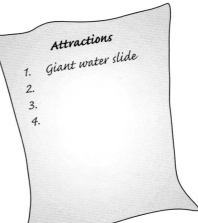

Now sketch your poster, noting on it what images and features you would use.

Summary

- Even in 'simple' posters, you can 'twist' language to make a product stand out (see page 84).
- Colour is a very powerful tool in creating atmosphere and image (see page 84).
- Layout can help to create ideas about a product (see page 85).

D2 Thoughts on-line ▶ ▶ ▶

D2 Thoughts on-line

Let's investigate...

- What features can an on-line review offer that a magazine review can't?
- How do you write a balanced review?

Objectives	
Word	
Sentence	2, 8
Reading	11
Writing	7, 12, 13, 15, 16, 17
Speaking/Listening	12

▶ Starting points: the dash

The dash is a useful punctuation mark. It can be used to:

- Show a break in a sentence where a speaker hasn't been able to finish what they were saying or has been interrupted.

> Debbie: Look! It's the –
>
> Matt: Oh no. You mean –
>
> Debbie: Yes! The police.

- Show missing words or letters.

> 3) Fill in the gap: an email is a form of – media.

- Show that an idea has been tagged onto a sentence – as an extra, if you like.

> The trip was great – and the shopping even better!

You must be careful not to overuse the dash, but it can be useful, especially in less formal writing, for example in electronic communication.

2.1

Work with a friend to write and perform a short scene where one character can't finish their sentences because they either get interrupted or – !

You could complete the one with Matt and Debbie above, if you want.

Look out for the use of the dash in the review opposite.

Reading source: film review: Spiderman

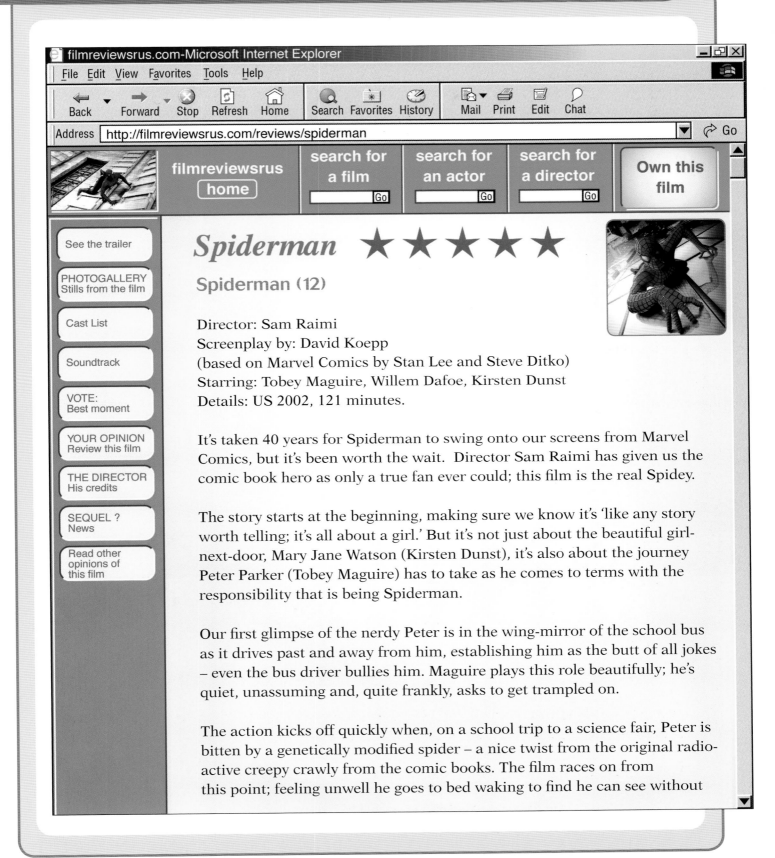

filmreviewsrus.com-Microsoft Internet Explorer

File Edit View Favorites Tools Help

Back Forward Stop Refresh Home Search Favorites History Mail Print Edit Chat

Address http://filmreviewsrus.com/reviews/spiderman Go

filmreviewsrus [home] | search for a film [Go] | search for an actor [Go] | search for a director [Go] | **Own this film**

- See the trailer
- PHOTOGALLERY Stills from the film
- Cast List
- Soundtrack
- VOTE: Best moment
- YOUR OPINION Review this film
- THE DIRECTOR His credits
- SEQUEL ? News
- Read other opinions of this film

Spiderman ★ ★ ★ ★ ★

Spiderman (12)

Director: Sam Raimi
Screenplay by: David Koepp
(based on Marvel Comics by Stan Lee and Steve Ditko)
Starring: Tobey Maguire, Willem Dafoe, Kirsten Dunst
Details: US 2002, 121 minutes.

It's taken 40 years for Spiderman to swing onto our screens from Marvel Comics, but it's been worth the wait. Director Sam Raimi has given us the comic book hero as only a true fan ever could; this film is the real Spidey.

The story starts at the beginning, making sure we know it's 'like any story worth telling; it's all about a girl.' But it's not just about the beautiful girl-next-door, Mary Jane Watson (Kirsten Dunst), it's also about the journey Peter Parker (Tobey Maguire) has to take as he comes to terms with the responsibility that is being Spiderman.

Our first glimpse of the nerdy Peter is in the wing-mirror of the school bus as it drives past and away from him, establishing him as the butt of all jokes – even the bus driver bullies him. Maguire plays this role beautifully; he's quiet, unassuming and, quite frankly, asks to get trampled on.

The action kicks off quickly when, on a school trip to a science fair, Peter is bitten by a genetically modified spider – a nice twist from the original radio-active creepy crawly from the comic books. The film races on from this point; feeling unwell he goes to bed waking to find he can see without

Continued ▶ ▶ ▶

glasses, has muscles and is able to climb walls and ceilings. Even more impressive, he is able to shoot silky webs from his wrists.

The scenes depicting his growing awareness of his powers are sensitive and funny – these are when we bond with Peter. The script and Maguire's spot-on acting create someone anyone can identify with; Peter Parker is a modern day Everyman. His joy and wonder at his new skills is nicely balanced by moments of real comedy, for example when he is learning to shoot webs or his Aunt Mary reprimands him, 'You're not Superman, you know.'

This film is not just an exciting action adventure following the lines of 'Batman' and 'Superman', it is also a journey of self-discovery where characters mature and develop and Peter learns the truth of his Uncle Ben's words: 'With great power comes great responsibility'.

It was worth the wait.

NOW:

read other opinions of this film

YOUR OPINION
Review this film yourself

I like this, what else will I like?

▶ **Reading focus:** have you understood?

2.2

Discuss these questions with a friend and then write the answers in full sentences.

- What star rating has this film been given; what does this tell us?
- What are the three categories you can use for searching?
- What buttons encourage the reader to become more involved?
- Who plays Spiderman/Peter Parker?
- How has the spider that bites Peter been changed from the original? Why do you think the film made this change?

Writing: modelling how it's done

The format of the extract you have just read is a web page, but within it there is a film review.

Let's look at the web page first.

The interactive features of the web page means it offers more than a film review in a paper magazine.

Extras

You can see photos of the actors and watch the trailer or clips from the film.

Links

You can follow a link to find out about an actor or the director. This will have links to other films actors have appeared in, or fan-sites about them.

Practical features

You can search for information and reviews about other films, actors and directors.

Interactivity

You can interact with the review/web site.
You can vote on the film, review it and read reviews written by other readers.

Continued

However, the written review uses writing features you should recognise.

Opening statement summarises the opinion

This shows us the writer is confident, which in turn makes us more likely to trust him/her.

Opinion is clear, but doesn't go over the top

It appears balanced and thoughtful because it gives reasons for its ideas. However, the reviewer might have been less thoughtful if he or she had hated the film!

Establishes self as expert

We are told the facts, figures and details. This adds to the authority of the reviewer.

There is a sprinkling of informal, chatty language

This makes the reviewer believable – like a friend chatting to us, although he or she does have clear opinions. Spiderman 'swings' onto our screens, Peter is described as 'nerdy' and the reviewer has no sympathy for him at the beginning, saying he deserves to get 'trampled'.

2.3

Your turn!

Design a simple review web page. Include a review of a film or TV programme you have seen recently.

You will need to plan both separately, then put them together.

> ### Plan for web page
> - Sketch the layout
> - Include links and images
>
> ### Plan for review
> - Follow the model you have just read
> - Summarise the plot simply and quickly with a key moment mentioned (not the end!)
> - Include views on the characters or actors
> - Sum up your own feelings
>
> ### Remember
> - You are the expert – make it sound as if you are
> - Have a clear opinion, but back it up with evidence
> - Use chatty, but accurate language

Summary

- New media such as web pages offer interactive features that can make the reading experience more enjoyable (see page 89).
- Practical features such as search facilities help make on-line reviews easy to use (see page 89).
- Facts, figures and details help to establish the writer as an expert (see page 90).
- Informal or conversational (colloquial) language can make the reviewer seem like a well-informed friend (see page 90).
- Reviews give a summary of the story, key moments and the reviewer's opinion (see page 90).

D3 Fun in the sun?

D3 Fun in the sun?

Let's investigate...

- What techniques does a holiday brochure use to sell a holiday?
- How does a newspaper review describe a disaster holiday?
- How do you analyse two texts?

Objectives	
Word	6, 7
Sentence	4, 9
Reading	2, 7, 10, 11, 12
Writing	3, 16, 17
Speaking/Listening	

▶ Starting points: positive and negative words

3.1

These words describe an event or experience. List them with the most positive at the top and the most negative at the bottom.

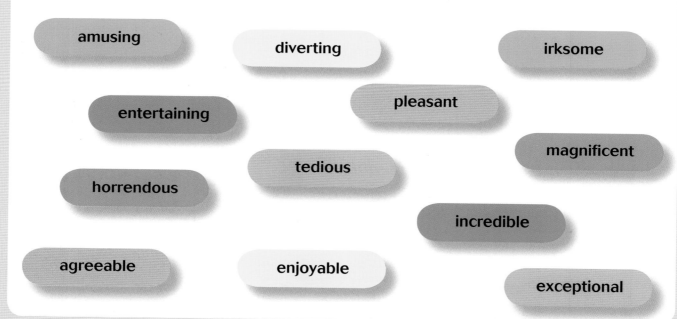

amusing

diverting

irksome

entertaining

pleasant

magnificent

tedious

horrendous

incredible

agreeable

enjoyable

exceptional

3.2

Now challenge a friend!

Find ten words to describe a journey – you might like to use a thesaurus to help you (make sure you include both positive and negative words). Mix them up and ask your friend to put them in order (most positive at top). Then read the texts on pages 93 and 94.

Reading: text 1

Sunville:
the perfect resort for the perfect holiday

A silver sandy beach, glittering blue sea and luxurious accommodation makes Sunville the top resort it is. Who could resist its many attractions? Whether you want to be pampered by the pool or surfing in the sea, this is the place for you.

First-time visitors to Sunville are always overwhelmed by the friendly welcome they receive, something the locals take pride in. We are delighted to be able to offer you the following holiday of a lifetime.

Hotel Sunville

Situated within easy walking distance of the beautiful beach, this luxury hotel provides an ideal base for your holiday. Guests stay in brand new suites that have every facility to hand. The only drawback is you won't want to leave!

Reading: text 2

No Sun and No Fun

'The perfect resort for the perfect holiday', the brochure promised.

OK, so perhaps I was a little naïve to expect what I was sold, but 'perfect' couldn't be further from the truth.

I arrived in Sunville eagerly expecting my 'friendly welcome'. Would there be music? Flowers? A feast? Actually, none of the above. I got off the transfer coach to a gormless bloke called Tom with a clipboard.

'This is Sunville?' I asked, making it clear I was a first-time visitor and therefore eligible for the aforementioned friendly welcome. 'Ummm,' he replied, and told me to wait.

And wait I did, for three hours for another coach to arrive and deposit more excited holiday-makers, looking forward to their week of luxury.

I can't actually bring myself to describe everything that went wrong on this holiday, needless to say my experience didn't

match the one outlined in the brochure. The beach was 'silver sand', but it was artificial and only thirty-metres long – a giant sandbox really. The sea was 'glittering blue', but you couldn't get near it because of the extensive building works. Diggers were at work all day and night, their noise drowning out all chance of relaxation or conversation. And as for sunbathing? Well you could sunbathe by the pool if you didn't mind lying by a puddle in the middle of a construction site. Not

something I'd recommend.

As for the hotel accommodation? Words can only just begin to describe how terrible this was. In fact, I'll leave it to your imagination – just make sure you're never tempted to find out for real.

Helen Cadwell went on a week's package holiday to Sunville (arranged through Nathan's Travel, London). N.B. The views expressed in this article are that of the author, and not necessarily representative of this newspaper.

Reading focus: have you understood?

3.3

- What sort of holiday does the brochure describe?
- What sort of holiday does Helen Cadwell actually experience?
- What is the purpose of the brochure extract?
- What is the purpose of the newspaper extract?
- What does the final 'N.B.' sentence after Helen's article mean, and why has the newspaper included it?

Writing: modelling how it's done

Look at this comparison table, which describes the two pieces.

FEATURE	Brochure	Article
Title and/ or slogan	*'Sunville: the perfect resort for the perfect holiday'.* Sums up the image and atmosphere the entry is trying to create.	*'No sun and no fun'.* Tells us straightaway what the article's point of view is.
Purpose	To persuade people to book a holiday.	To report on the holiday, and entertain readers with lively description.
Language	Use of adjectives and noun phrases – *'silver sandy beach'*, *'glittering blue sea'.* These bring the resort to life.	*'a giant sandbox'*; *'gormless bloke'*; phrases like these contrast with those in the brochure.
Style	*'overwhelmed by the friendly welcome'*; *'locals take pride in'*; suggests a personal touch.	*'Once upon a time … .'* and *'I arrived in Sunville … .'* gives this a storytelling feel. It's also quite personal.
Information (factual?)	*'easy walking distance'*; *'ideal base'*; *'brand new suites'*; seem factual, therefore believable.	*The beach was 'silver sand' but … .'* This is evidence to back up what is said, and quotes the original information from the article.
Special features	Rhetorical question used to persuade: *'Who could resist its many attractions?'*	1. Leaving things to the imagination: *'Words can only just begin to describe … .'* – this hints at the horror, but make sure you use this technique sparingly. 2. Questions are used humorously with a punchline; *'Would there be music? Flowers? A feast? Actually, none of the above.*

3.4 Your turn! ▶ ▶ ▶

Your turn!

Using the table above, write a comparison in full sentences of the two texts.
Explain how and why these texts give such a different impression of Sunville.
You can use the writing frame below, or write your own comparison piece.

▶ Writing frame

The texts give different impressions of Sunville because they are written for different purposes.

Text 1 is a ———————————— and it aims to ————————————— .

Text 2 is a ———————————— and it aims to ————————————— .

This affects the perspective they take, and the end result.
Text 1 is a holiday brochure, and so is not legally allowed to lie. However, it tries to make the holiday seem as good as possible. It does this by …

Text 2 is a personal report, and expresses a personal opinion. It tries to inform, but has also been written to entertain. It does this by …

Overall, I find Text ———— more believable because …

Challenge

3.5

Imagine you have been on the holiday Helen Cadwell described.

Write a letter of complaint to the holiday company. Look at your work in Unit B2 on page 37 to help you with letters of complaint.

> 345 Links Road,
> Winchester,
> Hants SO22 7XS
>
> Dear Sir/Madam,
>
> I have just returned from a holiday to Sunville ...

Summary

- Two texts on the same topic or theme can use different skills, and have different purposes (see page 96).
- A product's image and atmosphere can be established by the title and slogan (see page 96).
- Adjectives can be used in very persuasive ways to bring words to life (see page 96).
- Listing details can make writing seem factual, and therefore more trustworthy (see page 96).
- The storytelling technique can make a recount seem more personal and real (see page 96).
- Evidence proves you know what you are talking about (see page 97).

D4 Bad ads ▶ ▶ ▶

D4 Bad ads

Let's investigate...

- What is advertising used for?
- How does it work?

Objectives	
Word	1
Sentence	9
Reading	12
Writing	3, 13
Speaking/Listening	

▶ Starting points: qualifiers

Advertisers often make their products sound better or stronger than something else. This means that qualifiers such as 'latest', 'clearer' etc, are used.

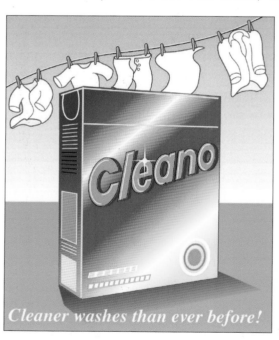

Cleano

Cleaner washes than ever before!

Fresher than a mountain spring from the deepest alpine rocks

O-Rock

The freshest taste you can get!

4.1

Here are some other common words used in adverts.

Write down each word and its qualifiers. The first one has been done for you.

1. fast *faster fastest*   2. smooth   3. thin   4. pure   5. good (be careful with this one!)

Reading source: Advertising – a bad business?

To some of us, adverts give a welcome break in between TV programmes by showing us glamorous people wearing beautiful clothes or driving fast cars. Billboard advertisements are something interesting to look at when we are travelling to school or work. Some adverts are so funny that we use their joke or catchphrase until the next one comes along. However, many people have complained that advertising is a bad influence, because it encourages us to want things that harm our health or the environment. Advertising also spends a lot of money on persuading us to buy certain products.

One good example of this is food. Many medical experts are worried about junk food in people's diets because it is usually high in saturated fat, sugar and additives. These are all things that cause killer diseases, such as obesity (serious weight problems), heart complaints, diabetes and cancers. Yet we only see happy, slim and fit people on junk food adverts, not overweight ones.

Reading focus: have you understood?

4.2

- Give two reasons why the writer thinks that advertising is a bad thing.
- What four reasons does the writer list for medical experts being worried about junk food?
- What is the effect of the phrase 'killer diseases'?

Writing: modelling how it's done

Writing: modelling how it's done

When you want to argue for or against something you need to:
- sound reasonable
- prove your point.

Look at how this has been done in this piece.

involves reader, seems friendly   *sounds positive; makes you sound reasonable*

To some of **us**, adverts give **a welcome break** in between TV programmes by showing us glamorous people wearing beautiful clothes or driving fast cars. Billboard advertisements are something interesting to look at when we are travelling to school or work. Some adverts are so funny that we use their joke or catchphrase until the next one comes along. **However**, many people have complained that advertising is a bad influence, because it encourages us to want things that harm our health or the environment. Advertising also spends a lot of money on persuading us to buy certain products.

One good example of this is food. **Many medical experts** are worried about junk food in people's diets because it is usually high is saturated **fat, sugar and additives**. These are all things that cause **killer diseases**, such as obesity (serious weight problems), heart complaints, diabetes and cancers. Yet we only see happy, slim and fit people on junk food adverts, not overweight ones.

introduces negative side in a thoughtful way

list suggests lots of evidence stacking up

punchy, emotive adjectives and nouns

evidence, swings argument (also, uses authority – the experts)

To sum up; when writing a piece arguing for or against something:
- appear thoughtful by understanding one side
- introduce your argument
- support it with evidence
- back up your main argument with strong adjectives, lists and expert opinions.

4.3

Your turn!

Now, you are going to write about a particular form of advertising – junk mail.

This is the mail that comes through your front door advertising a new product, or a service (such as the offer of a credit card).
Most people say that it is 'unsolicited'. This means they didn't ask for it. But is this true?

What do you think about junk mail? Is 'junk mail' a fair term?
Or is it only 'junk' if it advertises something we don't want?

Brainstorm all the good and bad things you can think of about junk mail.
Copy and complete this spidergram.

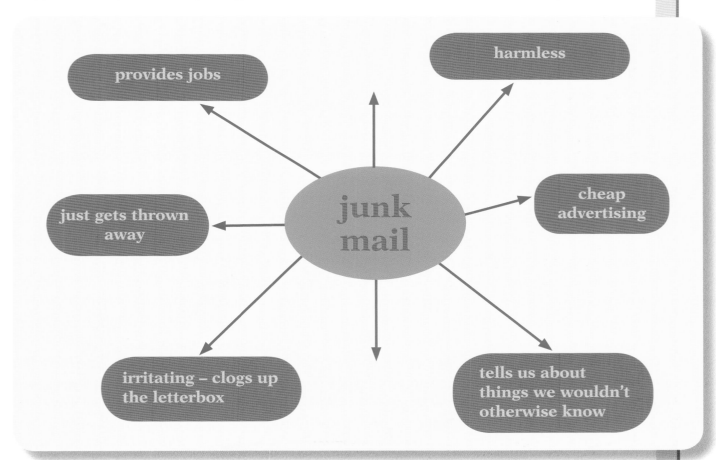

Now, decide if you are for or against junk mail.
Jot down a few good phrases or sentences you could use:

Examples:
- piles of multi-coloured paper
- a feast of good ideas to look through
- useless gadgets no one wants.

Continued ▶ ▶ ▶

4.4

Now, write your argument essay.

Use the ideas from your brainstorm. You will need to decide when and where to use the arguments.

For example: paragraph 1: say one good thing about junk mail

paragraph 2: introduce a bad thing about it

Use this frame, if you wish.

Introduction: one side of the argument.	Junk mail is …
What some people might think.	For some it provides …
The other side of the argument – YOUR point of view.	However,
Use some strong descriptions.	What is more, it …
Conclusion: finish off by summing up your main views.	So, as we can see, junk mail …

Summary

- Advertisements use qualifiers to make their product seem better than something else (see page 98).
- There are good and bad sides to advertising (see pages 99 and 102).
- Use a balanced and considered argument (see pages 100 and 102).
- Speak directly to your audience through personal pronouns such as 'us' and 'you' (see page 100).
- Use evidence to support your argument (see page 100).
- Add authority by using experts (see page 100).
- Add punch with emotive adjectives (see page 100).
- Lists and numbers can create an overwhelming effect (see page 100).

Media and ICT (Units 1–4)

1. Reading

The extracts I read were:
- Legoland advertisement
- 'Spiderman' film review
- Sunville holiday brochure
- Sunville newspaper article
- 'Bad Ads' extract.

2. Writing

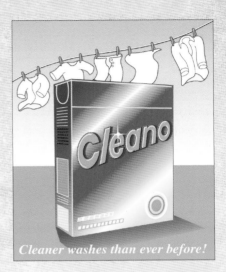

Cleaner washes than ever before!

In this section I have:
- designed a poster to advertise a new amusement park for teenagers
- written a short scene using dashes
- created a film or TV review web page
- written a film or TV review
- constructed an argument for or against junk mail
- written an analysis comparing two media texts.

3. Key learning

I have learned how to:
- manipulate language to make a product stand out
- use colour as a powerful tool in creating an image and atmosphere
- use layout to create ideas about a product
- include interactive features in the new media to help to engage and involve the audience
- use facts, figures and details to make a writer seem an expert
- use colloquial language to personalise writing
- not exaggerate opinions in presenting a considered argument
- present balanced and considered arguments to encourage people to listen
- use personal pronouns such as 'us' and 'you' to create a connection with the audience
- use qualifiers in advertisements to enhance their product.

Fresher than a mountain spring from the deepest alpine rocks

O-Rock

The freshest taste you can get!

4. Extension

I completed the following Challenge task:
- writing a letter of complaint to a holiday company.

SHAKESPEARE

E1 Introduction

Let's investigate...

- Who was Shakespeare?
- What are his plays about?
- How should you approach them?

Objectives	
Word	6
Sentence	
Reading	6, 14, 15
Writing	6
Speaking/Listening	

▶ Starting points: meet Shakespeare

Who was Shakespeare?

Shakespeare was born in 1564, the son of a glove-maker. When he died in 1616 he was a successful playwright. His plays had been performed before Queen Elizabeth and King James. But probably no one at the time thought that Shakespeare would one day be more famous than either of them.

What are his plays about?

The Shakespeare play you study will be one of three types:

Tragedy – murders, evil trickery, a tragic hero who dies.

Comedy – jokes, confusion, disguises, love, marriages.

History: based on real events, focusing on rulers and wars.

The plot

Most Shakespeare plots (storylines) can be understood using the STAR formula.

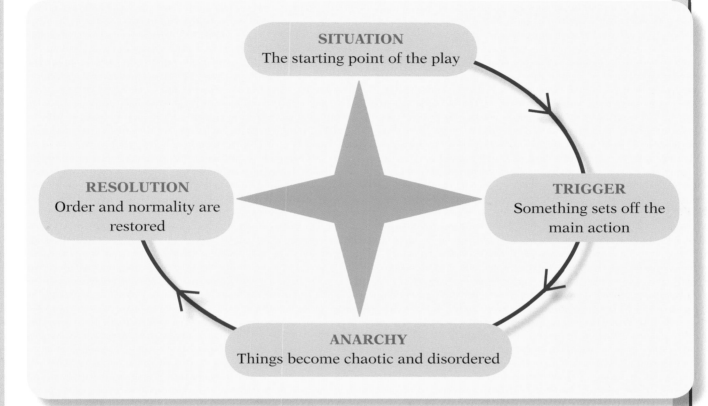

Even if you study only one scene, it will help if you know how it fits into the STAR formula within the play.

The characters

The characters' hopes, fears and ambitions create 'dramatic interest' and tension in the play. Even a single character may be torn between two things. For example, Macbeth wants to be King but does not want to kill King Duncan.

The language

Shakespeare wrote mostly in verse (poetry), and his English is almost 400 years old. But you will make sense of it if you follow these tips:
- You don't have to understand every word. Aim to get the general sense and the mood.
- Notice the punctuation. The end of a line may not be the end of a sentence.
- Look out for images (word pictures) suggesting ideas; for example, Shakespeare calls life a 'brief candle' (it doesn't last for long).
- Speak it aloud – it was written to be performed.

Reading: *Macbeth* Act 5, Scene 5

SEYTON: The queen, my lord, is dead.

MACBETH: She should have died hereafter;
           There would have been a time for such a word.
           Tomorrow, and tomorrow, and tomorrow,
           Creeps in this petty pace from day to day,
           To the last syllable of recorded time;
           And all our yesterdays have lighted fools
           The way to dusty death. Out, out, brief candle!
           Life's but a walking shadow, a poor player
           That struts and frets his hour upon the stage,
           And then is heard no more; it is a tale
           Told by an idiot, full of sound and fury,
           Signifying nothing.

Reading focus: have you understood?

1.1

Even with a short extract such as this, and knowing little about the play, you can find out quite a lot about the mood and feel.

Make a quick list of all the noun phrases (nouns + adjectives) in the speech. For example:

> **brief (adjective) + candle (noun)**

From this, plus any other information given in the extract, answer these questions:
- Which type of play is this extract most likely to come from?
- What is Macbeth's mood here?
- Where in the play would you expect this extract to come?

Challenge

1.2

Macbeth says that life is like a *'poor player'* (an actor) on the stage. He talks about how short the play (or life) is, and how the actor's words and actions mean *'nothing'*. This is an **extended metaphor** – taking a comparison and using it lots of times.

- Write an extended metaphor in which you describe school life as like a mountain climb. You could start:

	School life is like a mountain. At the start you gaze at the top and wonder if you'll ever get there ...

Summary

- Shakespeare wrote tragedies, comedies and histories (see page 104).
- Use the STAR formula to understand his plots (see page 105).
- The action is driven by what the characters want (see page 105).
- To read verse, follow the punctuation, look out for images, get the mood (see page 105).

E2 Call yourself a man?

E2 Call yourself a man?

Let's investigate...

- How can drama show tension between two people?
- How can their relationship develop?

Objectives	
Word	2, 5
Sentence	
Reading	12, 14
Writing	5, 14
Speaking/Listening	13, 14

▶ Starting points: spelling for Shakespeare

2.1

Below are some words you will need to understand and be able to spell. They will appear many times in the writing you have to do in class or in an exam.

Work with a partner.
- Decide between you what the words mean, if you can.
- Use a dictionary to check your ideas.
- Then test each other on the spellings.

character
dramatic
hero
image
irony
scene
soliloquy
tragedy
tragic
verse

Reading: *Macbeth* Act 1, Scene 7

Macbeth and his wife, Lady Macbeth, decide to murder King Duncan so that Macbeth can be King. Macbeth then changes his mind. His wife calls him a coward.

LADY MACBETH:	Was the hope drunk Wherein you dressed yourself? Hath it slept since? And wakes it now to look so green and pale At what it did so freely? From this time, Such I account thy love. Art thou afeard To be the same in thine own act and valour, As thou art in desire? Wouldst thou have that Which thou esteem'st the ornament of life, And live a coward in thine own esteem, Letting I dare not wait upon I would, Like the poor cat i'th'adage?
MACBETH:	Prithee, peace. I dare do all that may become a man; Who dares do more is none.
LADY MACBETH:	What beast was't then That made you break this enterprise to me? When you durst do it, then you were a man. And to be more than what you were, you would Be so much more the man. Nor time, nor place Did then adhere, and yet you would make both. They have made themselves and that their fitness now Does unmake you. I have given suck and know How tender 'tis to love the babe that milks me: I would, while it was smiling in my face, Have plucked my nipple from his boneless gums And dashed the brains out, had I so sworn as you Have done to this.
MACBETH:	If we should fail!
LADY MACBETH:	We fail! But screw your courage to the sticking-place, And we'll not fail.

GLOSSARY

afeard	*afraid*
art	*are*
durst	*dared to*
thine	*your*
thou	*you*
wouldst	*would*

Reading focus: have you understood?

2.2

Work with a partner. Find the lines that mean the following:

- You're like a drunk who wakes up with a hangover and is scared by what he's done.
- Are you too cowardly to aim for the one thing you really want?
- Anyone who does more than that is an animal.
- What beast inside you forced you to tell me about this plan?
- Now is the time and place to kill Duncan.
- Just be as brave as you can.

 # Writing: modelling how it's done

Speeches in Shakespeare are carefully structured. Look at this diagram showing how this speech is put together.

1. Lady Macbeth first taunts Macbeth for being a coward.

2. Then she questions his love for her, and reminds him how much he wants to be King. She says that when he planned to kill Duncan he was being a real man.

3. The climax is when she claims she would have killed her own baby if she'd sworn to do so.

4. Macbeth asks, 'What if we should fail?', and Lady Macbeth knows she's almost persuaded him.

5. She finishes by quickly saying that all he has to do is be brave.

2.3

Your turn!

Write a scene in which one person (A) is persuaded by someone else (B) to commit a crime.

Follow these stages:
1. A refuses to do it, and says why. (Make it clear what the crime is.)
2. B, angry and disappointed, tries to persuade A. (You could include a taunt here.)
3. A tries to argue back. (Include at least two good reasons for not doing it.)
4. B rejects this and the argument reaches a climax. (Perhaps a boast or a threat.)
5. A begins to give way, but still puts forward a reason not to commit the crime. (Like Macbeth's 'If we should fail?')
6. B drives home the advantage. (Perhaps 'Just leave it to me …'.)

Use this frame if you wish.

Make the persuader play on the other person's emotions – like Lady Macbeth. Write at least one speech for each of stages 1–6 as in the example below. Lay out your scene in the same way as the Macbeth extract.

A: I can't do it! It is …

B: What do you mean, you 'can't'? Why …

A: But …

B: That's ridiculous! If I …

A: OK, but what if …

B: Well, in that case …

Improving your work

2.4

Re-read the stages.

- Have you followed them properly?
- Is the 'emotional blackmail' convincing?

Challenge

2.5

An *adage* is a proverb, or saying. Lady Macbeth refers to the proverb, *'The cat would eat fish but would not wet her feet.'* This is like *'You can't make an omelette without breaking eggs.'*

Make up another two sayings like this. Complete this one.

You can't win the lottery without …

Summary

- There is drama in tension between two people (see pages 110–111).
- There is drama in how their relationship develops during the scene (see pages 110–111).

Let's investigate...

- How can you make a fight scene more interesting?
- How can a bad man also be a hero?

Objectives	
Word	7
Sentence	4
Reading	7, 14
Writing	5
Speaking/Listening	13, 14

▶ Starting points: shades of meaning

As you have seen in other units, you need to choose your words carefully to achieve the exact meaning you want.

In the extract you will read in this unit, Shakespeare describes a fight between two of the main characters, one of whom hates the other. But what they say to each other is not just 'Let's have a fight', as you will see.

3.1

The words below are all connected with 'fighting' but all have slightly different meanings.

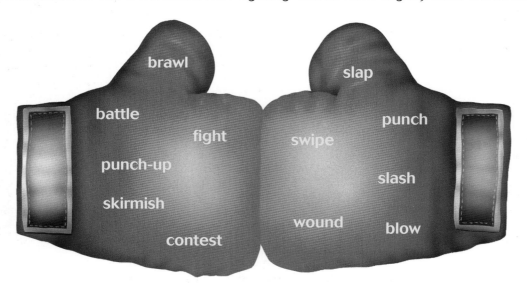

Explain the words you are clear about to a partner, and check the others in a dictionary, then put six of these words in sentences that show exactly what they mean.

Reading: *Macbeth* Act 5, Scene 8

Macbeth has killed Macduff's family. Macduff fights for Malcolm, the true King of Scotland, but he also wants revenge. Macduff forces Macbeth to fight. Macbeth thinks he is safe. Some Witches have told him he cannot be killed by any man born from a woman. But there is a surprise in store for him. As you read, think about how the fight would appear on stage.

MACDUFF:
Turn, hell-hound, turn.

MACBETH:
Of all men else I have avoided thee,
But get thee back, my soul is too much charged
With blood of thine already.

MACDUFF:
I have no words;
My voice is in my sword, thou bloodier villain
Than terms can give thee out.
Fight. Alarum.

MACBETH:
Thou losest labour.
As easy mayst thou the intrenchant air
With thy keen sword impress as make me bleed.
Let fall thy blade on vulnerable crests;
I bear a charmed life which must not yield
To one of woman born.

MACDUFF:
Despair thy charm,
And let the angel whom thou still hast served
Tell thee, Macduff was from his mother's womb
Untimely ripped.

MACBETH:
Accursed be that tongue that tells me so,
For it hath cowed my better part of man;
And be these juggling fiends no more believed
That palter with us in a double sense,
That keep the word of promise to our ear
And break it to our hope. I'll not fight with thee.

MACDUFF:
Then yield thee coward,
And live to be the show and gaze o'th'time.
We'll have thee, as our rarer monsters are,
Painted upon a pole and underwrit,
'Here may you see the tyrant.'

MACBETH:
I will not yield
To kiss the ground before young Malcolm's feet
And to be baited with the rabble's curse.
Though Birnam Wood be come to Dunsinane
And thou opposed being of no woman born,
Yet I will try the last. Before my body,
I throw my warlike shield. Lay on, Macduff,
And damned be him that first cries, 'Hold, enough!'

Exit Macbeth and Macduff, fighting.

GLOSSARY

intrenchant	*not capable of being cut*
cowed	*intimidated/overcome*
palter with	*trifle with*
vulnerable	*exposed to being harmed*
Dunsinane	*Macbeth's castle*

▶ Reading focus: have you understood?

3.2

Talk about the questions below with a partner. Then write your answers on your own. You may need to talk with your teacher about the rest of the play to understand all of the words and phrases in the speeches.

- What does Macduff threaten to do with Macbeth if he doesn't fight with him?
- What does Macbeth think about the 'juggling fiends' (the Witches) now?
- Why does Macbeth first refuse to fight Macduff?
- Why is Macbeth's 'charmed life' not safe from Macduff?
- What is your view of Macbeth at the end?

▶ Writing: modelling how it's done

Shakespeare makes the fight more interesting than a simple clash between enemies. Look at the events.
- Macbeth unexpectedly refuses to fight.
- He thinks he is safe.
- The 'twist': Macduff was not 'of woman born'.
- Macbeth's choice – fight to the death or be paraded as a 'monster'?
- Shakespeare shows that Macbeth is bad but brave – a hero.

What goes on in the minds of the fighters can be just as interesting as the action. For example, what is Macbeth thinking in this scene?

3.3 ♩

Your turn!

Write a fight scene with two characters.

There should be dialogue (speech), and either stage or camera directions.

You could choose a modern setting or an historical one. Here are some suggestions.

Make your scene interesting in the same ways that Shakespeare does.

- Set in the future, an investigator tracks down a human robot who has been taking over people's personalities after killing them.

- Set today, a woman customs official tracks down a drug smuggler to the edge of a cliff and orders him to surrender.

- Set in the past, a Roman slave escapes and tracks down the man who killed his family.

Follow this plan:
1. The first person (challenger) challenges the other (defender).
2. The defender refuses to fight, giving a reason.
3. They fight, but the defender thinks he/she is safe.
4. A twist reveals that the defender is not safe after all.
5. The challenger makes a threat that gives the defender a choice.
6. The scene ends with both showing bravery.

Improving your work

3.4

- Look at your choice of words.
  Does it show the way the two fighters feel about each other?

- Look back at how Macbeth and Macduff speak to each other.
  For example, Macduff calls Macbeth 'hell-hound'.

- See if you can improve your choice of words to show more feeling.

- Check that the wording of your scene directions (for example, 'he turns to face her') is accurate.

Summary

- Choose words carefully for exact meaning (see page 112).
- A fight scene is more interesting with unexpected twists (see page 114).
- The fighter's thoughts can be as interesting as the action (see page 114).

E4 Malvolio gets it wrong

Let's investigate...

- What is dramatic irony?
- How are misunderstandings funny?

Objectives	
Word	
Sentence	2, 3, 4
Reading	14, 15
Writing	5
Speaking/Listening	11, 12, 13, 14, 15

▶ Starting points: apostrophes in contractions

A contraction is a shortened phrase. An apostrophe is used to show where something has been missed out.

don't (do not)

they're (they are)

I'm (I am)

wouldn't (would not)

we'll (we will)

Contractions are used most often in speech; the full form often sounds too formal.
Use them less, or not at all, in formal writing.
Shakespeare often contracts a single word; for example, *smil'st* (*smilest*).

4.1

Rewrite the following using contractions.

1. I will have to use yours. Shaun's does not work.
2. Do not be afraid. It is only me.
3. You are the only one who will not be there.
4. Hardeep does not know if he has got the time.
5. Have not you got anything that is easy?

Reading: *Twelfth Night* Act 3, Scene 4

Dramatic irony

In *Twelfth Night*, Malvolio is Olivia's conceited chief servant. Maria is her maid. Maria and her friends have forged a letter 'from Olivia' to make Malvolio think Olivia is in love with him and wants him to wear 'cross-gartered' yellow stockings and smile a lot – although she is still upset about the death of her brother! In this extract, Malvolio quotes from the letter.

OLIVIA:	How now, Malvolio?
MALV.:	Sweet Lady, ho, ho!
OLIVIA:	Smil'st thou? I sent for thee upon a sad occasion.
MALV.:	Sad, lady? I could be sad: this does make some obstruction in the blood, this cross-gartering; but what of that? If it please the eye of one, it is with me as the very true sonnet is: 'Please one, and please all'.
OLIVIA:	Why, how dost thou, man? What is the matter with thee?
MALV.:	Not black in my mind, though yellow in my legs. It did come to his hands, and commands shall be executed. I think we do know the sweet Roman hand.
OLIVIA:	Wilt thou go to bed, Malvolio?
MALV.:	To bed? Ay, sweetheart, and I'll come to thee.
OLIVIA:	God comfort thee! Why dost thou smile so, and kiss thy hand so oft?
MARIA:	How do you, Malvolio?
MALV.:	At your request? Yes, nightingales answer daws!
MARIA:	Why appear you with this ridiculous boldness before my lady?
MALV.:	'Be not afraid of greatness': 'twas well writ.
OLIVIA:	What mean'st thou by that, Malvolio?
MALV.:	'Some are born great–'
OLIVIA:	Ha?
MALV.:	'Some achieve greatness–'
OLIVIA:	What say'st thou?
MALV.:	'And some have greatness thrust upon them.'
OLIVIA:	Heaven restore thee!
MALV.:	'Remember who commended thy yellow stockings–'
OLIVIA:	Thy yellow stockings?
MALV.:	'And wished to see thee cross-gartered.'
OLIVIA:	Cross-gartered?
MALV.:	'Go to, thou art made, if thou desir'st to be so–'
OLIVIA:	Am I made?
MALV.:	'If not, let me see thee a servant still.'
OLIVIA:	Why, this is very midsummer madness.

Reading focus: have you understood?

4.2

Discuss the questions below with a partner. Then write your answers on your own.

- What does the cross-gartering do to Malvolio?
- Olivia asks Malvolio if he wants to go to bed. What is the misunderstanding here?
- How does Olivia react to Malvolio in this scene?
- Which character knows most about what is going on?
- Read the lines that Malvolio quotes. What did the letter seem to promise him?

Writing: modelling how it's done

The comedy here comes from Shakespeare's use of 'dramatic irony'. This is when at least one character is unaware of something that the audience knows about. There is extra humour in this scene, because Maria knows what's going on and Malvolio *thinks* he does.

We laugh at Malvolio making a fool of himself.
This kind of comic misunderstanding is typical of Shakespeare.

4.3

Your turn!

Write a two-person scene that is funny because the characters have been tricked by a third person and do not know what is going on.

Choose from these two situations:
- A boy is tricked into believing a girl 'fancies' him. He thinks she's pretending she doesn't.
- A new employee tries to please the boss but has been set up by a workmate to get it wrong. (For example, the new employee has been told that the boss likes everyone to whistle and tell jokes.)

Follow this framework to write your scene.

Include the third person (the trickster) in your scene if you wish.

1. Person A speaks to Person B in a way that surprises Person B.
2. Person B replies, not encouraging Person A.
3. Person A tries to please Person B but gets it completely wrong.
4. Person B speaks and is completely misunderstood by A.
5. B thinks that A is mad or ill.

Improving your work

4.4

Re-read your scene. Ask yourself:
- Will it be clear to an audience what is going on?
- Can you improve on the choice of words to make it funnier?
- How could stage directions help to make it funnier?

Challenge: dramatic irony

4.5

Working with two other people, practise your scene and perform it to a small group. When you have finished, write 100 words on one person's performance other than your own, and what the strengths and weaknesses were.

4.6

If you know the story of *Twelfth Night* write down a list of three other scenes in which either one character – or the audience – knows the truth but another character doesn't.

Summary

- Apostrophes in contractions show where something is left out (see page 116).
- Contractions make speech or writing sound less formal (see page 116).
- Dramatic irony is when at least one character does not know what the audience knows (see page 118).
- Shakespeare's comedies are full of misunderstandings (see page 118).

E5 Comparing scenes

E5 Comparing scenes

Let's investigate...

- How does Shakespeare show two sides to a character?
- How do you compare two scenes?

Objectives	
Word	1, 3
Sentence	
Reading	7
Writing	3, 16
Speaking/Listening	13

▶ Starting points: possessive apostrophes

- An apostrophe shows possession. For one thing or person, it goes before the 's':

    The cat's whiskers   Malvolio's stockings

- For two or more things or people it goes after the 's':

    Eleven players' shirts   Steps' Greatest Hits

- Never use an apostrophe in 'its', as in 'I got its number.'
- Never use an apostrophe just because a word is plural, as in   **Bananas' for sale!**

5.1

Check back over two pages of your written work. Have you used apostrophes correctly?

5.2

Write four sentences using apostrophes as explained in the examples above.

Shakespeare often uses apostrophes to shorten words so that they have fewer syllables. This can help the rhythm of the speech, and make some words more fluent or punchy.

▶ Reading: *Henry V* Act 3, Scene 3

Two sides of a king

In the first scene, Henry stands outside the walls of a French town and warns its people what will happen if they do not surrender.

Reading: *Henry V* Act 3, scene 3 (continued)

HENRY: How yet resolves the governor of the town?
This is the latest parle we will admit:
Therefore to our best mercy give yourselves;
Or like to men proud of destruction
Defy us to our worst: for, as I am a soldier,
A name that in my thoughts becomes me best,
If I begin the batt'ry once again,
I will not leave the half-achiev'd Harfleur
Till in her ashes she lie buried.
The gates of mercy shall be all shut up,
And the flesh'd soldier, rough and hard of heart,
In liberty of bloody hand shall range
With conscience wide as hell, mowing like grass
Your fresh-fair virgins and your flow'ring infants.
What is it then to me, if impious war,
Array'd in flames like to the prince of fiends,
Do, with his smirch'd complexion, all fell feats
Enlink'd to waste and desolation?

GLOSSARY

array'd	*dressed*
batt'ry	*cannon fire*
flesh'd	*trained in killing*
impious	*unholy*
parle	*talk/negotiation*
smirch'd	*soiled/smeared*

Reading: *Henry V* Act 5, Scene 2

The second extract is set in a French palace. Henry has beaten the French and wants to marry the French princess. You do not need to understand the French: Katherine is just checking that she understands Henry's English. Her maid Alice translates for her.

HENRY:	Fair Katharine, and most fair, Will you vouchsafe to teach a soldier terms Such as will enter at a lady's ear And plead his love-suit to her gentle heart?
KATHARINE:	Your majesty shall mock at me; I cannot speak your England.
HENRY:	O fair Katharine! if you will love me soundly with your French heart, I will be glad to hear you confess it brokenly with your English tongue. Do you like me, Kate?
KATHARINE:	Pardonnez-moi, I cannot tell vat is 'like me'.
HENRY:	An angel is like you, Kate, and you are like an angel.
KATHARINE:	Que dit-il? Que je suis semblable a les anges? *
ALICE:	Oui, vraiment, sauf votre grace, ainsi dit-il. **
HENRY:	I said so, dear Katharine, and I must not blush to affirm it.
KATHARINE:	O bon Dieu! Les langues des hommes sont pleines de tromperies. ***
HENRY:	What says she, fair one? That the tongues of men are full of deceits?
ALICE:	Oui; dat de tongues of de mans is be full of deceits: dat is de princess.
HENRY:	The princess is the better Englishwoman. I' faith, Kate, my wooing is fit for thy understanding; I am glad thou canst speak no better English; for if thou couldst, thou wouldst find me **such a plain king that thou wouldst think I had sold my farm to buy my crown.**

GLOSSARY

vouchsafe *agree/grant*

* [What does he say? That I look like the angels?]
** [Yes indeed, that's what he said.]
*** [Oh good Lord! The tongues of men are full of deceit.]

> Reading focus: have you understood?

5.3

Discuss the questions below with a partner. Then write your answers on your own.

- The first scene is set outside a town under siege; the second is in a French palace. How do these settings fit the mood in each case?
- What is Henry like in each extract?
- What differences in style are there? For example, which uses more verse?
- How are images (word pictures) used in each extract?

> Writing: modelling how it's done

If you are asked to look at two different scenes from the same play, ask yourself the kind of questions you looked at in 5.3. You need to think about:

Plot
How is one scene connected to the other through the story? (Does one scene lead to another? Sometimes, scenes can mirror each other.)

Style
Is verse or prose used? Is there imagery? If so, what does it suggest? (The imagery in the first extract suggests savage destruction.)

Setting
How it fits, or creates, atmosphere.

Characters
Similarities and differences.

Mood
Of the extract and of the characters. (For example, Henry is playful in the second extract.)

Continued ▶ ▶ ▶

5.4

Your turn!

Compare the two extracts. But before you begin, re-read them carefully.

Then, write a paragraph on each of the headings given in 'Writing' on page 123.

Follow the hints below:

1

Setting

- What are the settings?
- What sort of behaviour would you expect in each?

2

Characters

- Who are the characters in each scene?
- Who is 'in charge'? Who has the most power?
- How is Henry different in each scene?
- How is he the same?
- How does he treat Katharine?

3

Mood

- What is Henry trying to do in each scene and how does this affect the mood? Give an example from each scene – for example a threat from the first scene and a joke or something romantic from the second.

4

Style

- Why does Shakespeare use verse in the first extract and prose in the second? (Hint: how easy would it be to put the second extract into verse?)
- Describe the effect of imagery (word pictures) in the first extract: *'gates of mercy'*, *'mowing like grass'* and *'impious war'* like the *'prince of fiends'* and *'dressed in flames'*. In the second extract, what does Henry say Katharine is like? Why do you think he says this?

5

Plot

- How is the second scene linked to the first?
- Could the second scene have happened if Henry had lost to France in the battles that take place?

Improving your work

5.5

- Have you written in full sentences?
- Have you indented new paragraphs?
- Have you used quote-marks (inverted commas) for quotations from the scenes?

Challenge

5.6

When we talk about people having 'two sides' to their characters we usually mean a good and bad side. But sometimes it might be that they have a public face (what they show to the outside world) and a private face (what they show to people who know them, such as family).

We still use the word 'side' when we talk about people.
What do you think these expressions mean?

'She's got a dark side.'

'She's got no side to her at all.'

'Don't get on the wrong side of him!'

'He always looks on the bright side of things.'

Summary

- Use apostrophes to show possession, but don't use in ordinary plurals (see page 120).
- A character may have several 'sides' (see page 125).
- To compare scenes, look at setting, character, mood, style and plot (see page 123).

Let's investigate...

- How can a Shakespeare story be modernised?
- How can bad news be dramatically interesting?
- How do you write 'in role'?

Objectives	
Word	7
Sentence	
Reading	7, 9, 14, 15, 16
Writing	5
Speaking/Listening	12, 13

 ## Starting points: shades of meaning

6.1

The words and phrases in each column below have slightly different meanings.

loves	hates
is fond of	detests
likes	dislikes
worships	loathes
is attracted to	is revolted by
adores	despises

Put three words from each column in sentences that show what they mean.

Reading: the bad news (extract A)

Like the starter exercise, the following extracts are all about love and hate. (A) is from
Romeo and Juliet Act 5, Scene 1. Romeo (a Montague) has killed Juliet's cousin
(a Capulet), who murdered his best friend. Romeo now hears that Juliet is dead. She has
actually taken a sleeping potion, but Balthasar (who brings the news) does not know this.

Extract A

ROMEO: If I may trust the flattering truth of sleep,
My dreams presage some joyful news at hand.
My bosom's lord sits lightly in his throne,
And all this day an unaccustom'd spirit
Lifts me above the ground with cheerful thoughts.
I dreamt my lady came and found me dead–
Strange dream, that gives a dead man leave to think–
And breath'd such life with kisses in my lips,
That I reviv'd and was an emperor.
Ah me! How sweet is love itself possess'd,
When but love's shadows are so rich in joy!

Enter Balthasar, booted

News from Verona! How now, Balthasar?
Dost thou not bring me letters from the friar?
How doth my lady? Is my father well?
How doth my lady Juliet? That I ask again,
For nothing can be ill if she be well.

BALTHASAR: Then she is well, and nothing can be ill;
Her body sleeps in Capel's monument,
And her immortal part with angels lives.
I saw her laid low in her kindred's vault,
And presently took post to tell it you.
O pardon me for bringing these ill news,
Since you did leave it for my office, sir.

ROMEO: Is it e'en so? Then I defy you, stars!
Thou know'st my lodging: get me ink and paper,
And hire post-horses. I will hence tonight.

GLOSSARY

import	*threaten*
office	*duty*
presage	*predict/promise*
vault	*tomb*

Continued

BALTHASAR: I do beseech you, sir, have patience:
Your looks are pale and wild and do import
Some misadventure.

ROMEO: Tush, thou art deceiv'd;
Leave me, and do the thing I bid thee do.
Hast thou no letters to me from the friar?

BALTHASAR: No, my good lord.

ROMEO: No matter; get thee gone,

And hire those horses: I'll be with thee straight.

[Exit Balthasar]

Well, Juliet, I will lie with thee tonight.

▶ Reading: the bad news (extract B)

Extract B is from the film *West Side Story*.

Tony (a member of the Jets gang) has murdered Maria's brother (Puerto Rican, a member of the Sharks gang), who killed his best friend. Tony waits for Maria at Doc's store. Doc has just heard that Maria is dead. You may see the similarity with *Romeo and Juliet*.

One of the gangs from *West Side Story*.

Extract B

11.50 p.m. The cellar
Cramped: a box or crate; stairs leading to the
drugstore above; a door to the outside.
Tony is sitting on a crate, whistling 'Maria'
as Doc comes down the stairs, some [dollar]
bills in his hand.

TONY: Make a big sale?

DOC: No.

TONY: *(Taking the money that Doc is*
holding) Thanks. I'll pay you back
as soon as I can.

DOC: Forget that.

TONY: I won't; I couldn't. Doc, you know
what we're going to do in the
country, Maria and me? We're
going to have kids and we'll name
them all after you, even the girls.
Then when you come to visit–

DOC: *(Slapping him)* Wake up! *(Raging)*
Is that the only way to get through
to you? Do just what you all do?
Bust like a hot-water pipe?

TONY: Doc, what's gotten–

DOC: *(Overriding angrily)* Why do you live
like there's a war on? *(Low)* why do
you kill?

TONY: I told you how it happened, Doc.
Maria understands. Why can't
you?

DOC: I never had a Maria.

TONY: *(Gently)* I have, and I'll tell you
one thing, Doc. Even if it only
lasts from one night to the next,
it's worth the world.

DOC: That's all it did last.

TONY: What?

DOC: That was no customer upstairs,
just now. That was Anita. *(Pause)*
Maria is dead. Chino found out
about you and her – and shot her.

(A brief moment. Tony looks at Doc,
stunned, numb. He shakes his head, as
though he cannot believe this. Doc holds
out his hands to him, but Tony backs away,
then suddenly turns and runs out the door.
As he does, the set flies away and the stage
goes dark. In the darkness, we hear Tony's
voice.)

TONY: Chino? Chino? Come and get me,
too, Chino.

Reading focus: have you understood?

6.2

Discuss these questions; they deal with both extracts. Then write your answers.

- What mood is Romeo in before Balthasar arrives?
- What mood is Tony in before Doc slaps him?
- How do Romeo and Tony react to the news they receive?
- Re-read the final lines of each extract. What does each mean?
- How are the two extracts different in style? Why?

Writing: modelling how it's done

Writing: modelling how it's done

In both cases someone expecting good news gets bad news. In both cases the audience knows that the bad news is a mistake: Juliet and Maria are still alive. Balthasar and Doc do not know this.

This dramatic irony (when the audience knows something that at least one character does not know) makes what happens more tragic. As an audience, we are also interested in how the main character reacts, and what happens as a result of their actions.

6.3

Your turn!

Imagine you are one of the characters.

After the scene, an interviewer asks you:
- How do you feel about all that's happened?'
- Do you have any regrets?

- Who is to blame?
- What will you do now?

Write 'in role' about your thoughts and feelings. Use the questions as a rough guide. Here are some possible beginnings:

DOC:	Tony's a good boy at heart. How did he do this terrible thing? Kids today …
TONY:	How can I live without Maria? Maybe this is what I deserve. If only …
BALTHASAR:	I'm worried about Romeo. If only I'd had good news. Now he might …
ROMEO:	The world makes no sense. I can't believe what's happened. Why …

Show that you understand what has happened, and what the character must feel like now.
It can be effective to use one or two short quotes, for example:

> **BALTHASAR:** It was terrible to see Romeo looking so eager and hopeful, asking me 'How doth my lady Juliet?' I could hardly bear to tell him …

You don't have to write in Shakespearean or American English. Concentrate on getting inside the character.

Summary

- Bad news can be dramatically interesting (see page 130).
- Dramatic irony is when the audience knows something a character does not know (see page 130).
- To write 'in role', imagine you are the character (see page 130).

Shakespeare (Units 1–6)

1. Reading

The extracts I read were:
- *Macbeth*
- *Twelfth Night*
- *Henry V*
- *Romeo and Juliet*
- *West Side Story.*

2. Writing

In this section I have written:
- a scene based on persuasion
- an interesting fight scene
- a comic scene based on dramatic irony
- a comparison of two scenes from *Henry V*
- an account 'in role' as a character in *Romeo and Juliet* or *West Side Story*.

3. Key learning

I have learned how to:
- approach Shakespeare's plots, characters and language
- use key spellings for writing about Shakespeare
- understand and use dramatic tension
- choose between words with similar meanings
- make a fight scene more interesting
- use apostrophes in contractions and for possession
- use dramatic irony for humour
- compare scenes within a play and in different plays
- write 'in role' as a character.

4. Extension

I completed the following Challenge tasks:
- writing an extended metaphor
- making up 'sayings'
- performing a comic scene and commenting on someone else's performance
- using the word 'side' to describe people.

 **Reading in the test situation**

Let's investigate...

- How do you understand test-style questions?
- What reading skills do you need in the test situation?

Objectives	
Word	
Sentence	4
Reading	1, 2
Writing	1, 3
Speaking/Listening	

► Starting points: common reading questions

1.1

Here are four common, different style reading questions that appear in test situations.

a) Find the phrase in paragraph 1 that shows Mrs Malone is very angry. ◄
b) Explain how Mrs Malone felt at the end of the story.
c) Mrs Malone is referred to as 'hard as a rock of ice' in the third paragraph. Explain why the writer chose this phrase and what it tells us.
d) List three things from the passage that Mrs Malone does that annoy her daughter.

Which of these would you think is likely to be the **most difficult** question?
Which do you think likely to be the **easiest**?

Even without reading the passage, it is likely that 'c' will be the most challenging. Because:

- The question is long and in several parts.
- It refers to a quotation (an actual line from the piece) that you have to find.
- You have to explain why the writer chose this phrase.
- You have to write down what the phrase tells us, the reader.

It is likely that 'a' is the easiest. Because:

- The question is short and has only one part.
- 'Angry' is easy to understand. You should be able to find the bit of the text where someone is behaving in this way.

In other words, questions in test situations are all very different. But it is important to know which are easy and which are more difficult.

Reading

This text comes from the reading section of an English exam. Read it carefully.

As I walk onto the estate, the first thing that assaults my eyes is the shell of a burnt out car, lying forlorn by the side of the road. Two children who can't be more than six or seven, are taking it in turns to throw stones through the hollow rectangle where the windscreen once was. It is awful. Walking on, I am saddened by the boarded up houses, with streaks of black, like scars, down their brickwork. A radio booms out bass notes, and a baby cries somewhere.

But then, as I turn the corner, I am faced with an oasis of green; a large circular area of grass, with a newly-painted swing planted firmly in the middle. This little island is surrounded by a neat iron railing, and several polished wooden benches. Four or five children are playing happily on the climbing frame, and two mothers watch them from nearby. It is like stepping through the back of a wardrobe and finding a wonderful, whole new land behind it.

Shona Martin, *Estate Life*

Reading focus: have you understood?

1.2

Here are three possible questions that you might be asked about this text.
Do not write the answers down. First go through them with a partner and discuss them.
The marks for each question are given in brackets.

a) In the first paragraph, what is the 'first thing' that meets the writer's eyes?   (1)
b) List two phrases used to describe the grassy area in the second paragraph.   (2)
c) The writer describes the houses as having 'scars' in the first paragraph.
   What effect is the writer trying to create?   (3)

Use the marks for each question to judge how long you spend on each one.
A question worth one mark should take half the time of a question worth two.

▶ Writing: modelling how it's done

So, what would be good responses to these questions?

Let's look at the most difficult question, the third one.

First of all, we need to break it down. We can underline or highlight the key parts.

> c) The writer describes **the houses** as having 'scars' in the **first paragraph.**
> What **effect** is the writer trying to **create**? (3)

In other words …

- The question refers to the houses, not the children, or the car.
- The word 'scars' is the key word, not any others.
- We are looking for the effect – what does the choice of this word rather than 'marks', for example, make us think of? (What is the writer creating?)

1.3

Here are three answers.

The scars on the houses are marks which don't make them look very nice.

The scars on the houses are like wounds. The writer is trying to get across the feeling that the houses almost have feelings, like people.

The scars on the houses are marks which don't make them look very nice. The writer is trying to make us feel that the estate is not a good place to live.

Which one of these is the best answer?

1.4

Here is another test-style question on the passage:

> How do the writer's feelings change when she finds the grassy play area on the estate? (5)
>
> **Consider:**
> - how she feels at the start
> - what has made her feel like this
> - how she feels when she sees the play area.

This is an even longer question. It has five marks, so you should try to write about half a page, and cover each of the bullet points listed under 'Consider'.

The process

1. First, select the key words from the question.
2. Now read quickly through the passage again.
3. Look for key words or phrases as evidence for your answer.
4. Now answer the question. Use this frame, if you wish.

At first, the writer feels
because
She says she
However, when she reaches the play area she describes it as
She thinks it is

Improving your work

1.5

Finished? Show your answer to a friend, and see whether you have both covered all the parts of the question. If not, re-do your answer quickly.

Summary

- Questions vary in style and difficulty (see page 132).
- Look at the number of marks to help you tell how much to write (see page 133).
- Use the key words in the title (see page 134).
- Where suitable, use evidence from the extract (see page 134).

F2 Reading and responding to Shakespeare scenes

Let's investigate...

- What, exactly, does 'compare' mean?
- How do I compare two scenes from a Shakespeare play?

Objectives	
Word	
Sentence	4
Reading	
Writing	10, 17
Speaking/Listening	
Drama	13

▶ Starting points: comparisons

2.1

Talk with a friend about what you did on Saturday – whether you enjoyed it or not, who you saw, and so on.

Now, talk about Sunday.

- **Did you do the same things?**
- **Did you do different things?**
- **Was it better, or worse than Saturday?**
- **Whom did you see? (the same people as on Saturday, or different people?)**
- **What were they like?**

These are the sorts of questions you might think about when writing about Shakespeare.

In your test, you will have to look at two different scenes.

These two scenes are really like the Saturday and Sunday you described.

They involve:
- **people (perhaps the same, perhaps different)**
- **feelings (perhaps happy, perhaps sad, perhaps angry)**
- **two different times in the play. They could be the same day (but morning or afternoon) or different days, even different years.**

Reading: *Macbeth* Act 1, Scene 7

Here are some notes made by a student about Lady Macbeth in two scenes from Shakespeare's play *Macbeth*.

Act 2, Scene 2: Macbeth has just murdered the King in order to become King himself.	Act 5, Scene 1: Macbeth has murdered some of his enemies, but his rivals are ganging up on him, and a big battle is coming.
• Lady Macbeth has had something to drink to give her courage. • She stays behind while her husband goes off to murder the King. • When he comes back, he is shaking with the thought of what he has done; she tries to get him to pull himself together. • She takes the daggers from him (he refuses to go back to the scene of the murder) and takes them back to the King's room. • She comes back with blood on her hands.	• A doctor and a lady-in-waiting watch Lady Macbeth at night. • She is sleepwalking. • She appears to be trying to wash her hands. • he talks about how much blood 'the old man' had in him. • She talks about the ghosts of people Macbeth has killed. • Four scenes later, she is dead.

Reading focus: have you understood?

2.2

Whether you know the play or not, discuss with a friend what differences in behaviour you can see between Lady Macbeth's actions in Act 2, Scene 2 and Act 5, Scene 1.

Writing: modelling how it's done ▶ ▶ ▶

Writing: modelling how it's done

What does the word 'compare' actually mean?

If you compare one thing, or person, or event, with another, you look for:
- the similarities
- the differences.

In comparing the two scenes from *Macbeth*, you could say they were similar because:
- they both had Lady Macbeth in them
- they were both about her feelings and behaviour, especially in relation to the murders her husband has done.

If you were playing the part of Lady Macbeth, you could show:
- how her behaviour changes from one scene to the next or
- how her behaviour is similar in both scenes.

For example:
Perhaps she is already beginning to feel guilty and terrified even in the first scene?
Perhaps she is already shocked when she looks at the blood on her hands?

In an assessment, you will be asked to find connections between scenes.

Connections means links.

In the two scenes mentioned, connections could be made between:

- the blood on Lady Macbeth's hands
- her attitude to the killings
- her courage, or fear (drinking and sleepwalking)
- the fact she is alone in one scene, but with her husband in the other
- our different feelings towards her (do we feel sorry for her in one scene, but not the other?)
- the actual lines in both scenes (you could look at what she says about the blood on her hands, what Macbeth says about the blood on his hands …).

In other words, connections could be made between:

- what actually happens in the scene
- who is in it
- what has happened just before it
- what is about to happen
- our feelings
- the character's feelings and behaviour
- other characters' feelings and behaviour
- the words spoken in the scenes.

2.3

Your turn!

Now choose any two scenes from a Shakespeare play you are studying.
These should be scenes in which at least one character appears in both.
Now make brief notes for all the points on the list above.

Summary

- Comparing scenes in plays is not that different from comparing real events in life (see page 136).
- Look for connections and links (see page 138).
- Prepare by making notes on those connections and links (see page 139).
- Don't forget what happens in the rest of the play (see page 139).

F3 Writing comparisons

F3 Writing comparisons

Let's investigate...

- How do you make sure your comparison writing is organised and clear?

Objectives	
Word	7, 8
Sentence	4
Reading	
Writing	10, 17
Speaking/Listening	

▶ Starting points

3.1

Discuss with a friend the difference in meaning between these two sentences.

> a) Lady Macbeth feels nothing to begin with, but feels guilty later.
>
> b) Lady Macbeth feels guilty as well as depressed.

Perhaps you said:

Sentence a) shows the difference between her feelings at the start of the play, and her feelings later.

Sentence b) shows her different feelings, but they are connected, which is why the writer uses 'as well as'.

As you have seen throughout this book, and in school, connecting or linking words and phrases such as these are very useful when writing comparisons about texts, people or events.

They help shape your writing and, as you have seen in other units, they act as signposts to the reader.

This is particularly important when your work is being read by an examiner who has never met you!

Reading

Here is someone writing about the two films *Harry Potter and the Philosopher's Stone* and *The Lord of the Rings*.

Harry Potter and *The Lord of the Rings* both deal with magic, other worlds and sorcery. However, they are very different in many ways. On the one hand, *Harry Potter* is light-hearted and quite funny, whereas *Lord of the Rings* is dark and serious. *Harry Potter* is also mainly about children, but *Lord of the Rings* deals more with adults, many of whom are not human. Moreover, *Lord of the Rings* is genuinely frightening. *Harry Potter*, in contrast, only has one really scary moment, which is when Voldemort appears in the forest.

Reading focus: have you understood?

3.2

List as many comparison or contrast words as you can find in this extract.
There are about seven of them (for example, 'however').

Writing: modelling how it's done ▶ ▶ ▶

Writing: modelling how it's done

3.3

To practise your comparisons and contrasts choose one of the topics from the list below:

- two films or videos you have seen
- two comedy programmes you have seen
- two books or stories you have read
- two scenes from Shakespeare you have studied
- two classes you have been to in school.

Write two paragraphs in which you compare the two things.
Try to use one word or phrase from each of these sections.

Similarities	like, in the same way, as well, also, moreover
Differences	on the other hand, whereas, unlike, in contrast, but

Revising evidence and quotations

Often, when you have to compare two texts, or characters, you have to provide evidence for what you say.

Remember:

Evidence can be just giving an example.

For example, if you say, *Harry Potter is a silly boy who always makes mistakes*, you need to support it with evidence.

You could say, *as can be seen when he makes the mistake of using magic on a non-wizard in Chapter X when ... .*

Or you could give a quotation.
Quotations are the actual lines from the text you have studied.

Lady Macbeth is already feeling the pressure in Act 2, Scene 2 of Macbeth, when she says 'that which hath made them drunk hath made me bold', meaning that she has been drinking the same drink she gave to the king's servants.

You must remember to put quotations inside inverted commas (or speech marks).

'... that which hath made them drunk hath made me bold ...'.

Challenge

3.4

Go back to the comparison you wrote in task 3.3. Check you have added evidence to support what you say.

If it is a book, add a quotation to support your points.

3.5

In some tests you will write about three different texts.

Here are descriptions of four other texts all connected to the *Harry Potter* or *The Lord of the Rings* reviews on page 141.

Can you identify any links?

> **Is Magic Real?**
>
> A newspaper article looking at magic in stories and whether it can be explained scientifically.

> **Director's Diary**
>
> Peter Jackson, director of *The Lord of the Rings*, describes a typical day on set.

> **Witches Alive!**
>
> A front page news story about two real teenage witches.

> **Bike review**
>
> Magazine which reviews the latest BMXs available for Christmas.

Summary

- Comparison words help shape your writing (see page 140).
- Use evidence and quotations to support what you say (see page 142).
- Always use inverted commas around quotations (see page 142).

Preparing for assessment (Units 1–3)

1. Reading

The extracts I read were:
- Shona Martin, *Estate Life*
- William Shakespeare, *Macbeth*
- *Harry Potter and the Philosopher's Stone* and
- *The Lord of the Rings* film review.

2. Writing

In this section I have written:
- a longer answer to a reading question (on *Estate Life*)
- notes on two Shakespeare scenes for comparison
- a longer comparison about two things of my choice.

3. Key learning

I have learned how to:
- understand the different types of question
- focus on the right parts of a question
- judge how much to write
- find connections and links between texts
- use comparison words in texts
- use evidence and quotations when writing.

4 Extension

I completed the following Challenge tasks:
- added quotations and evidence to my comparison work
- looked for links between texts.